Dee's Dishes

Denise Dwyer D'Errico

Dee's Dishes

Copyright © 2017 – Denise Dwyer D'Errico

All rights reserved.

All rights reserved. No part of this publication may be reproduced, distributed or transmitted in any form or by any means, including photocopying, recording, or other electronic or mechanical methods, without the prior written permission of the publisher, except in the case of brief quotations embodied in critical reviews and certain other non-commercial uses permitted by copyright law.

Formatting by Rik: Wild Seas Formatting (http://WildSeasFormatting.com)

Publisher's Note: This is a memoir and recipe collection. Names, characters, places, and brands may have been changed. Locales and public names are sometimes used for atmospheric purposes. Please note: sometimes people don't remember where their recipes came from. Their fourth generation special recipe may have come from the side of a box. I've indicated the source of a recipe, if known, and specified the derivatives. Any copying of recipes is unintentional. Finally, dear friends and family members have shared certain recipes with me, and I have honored them accordingly within.

Dee's Dishes / Denise Dwyer D'Errico —1st ed.

ISBN-13: 978-1542488921
ISBN-10: 1542488923

Dedication

With special fondness to my beloved family and friends and readers. You know who you are. Special thanks to friends and family who shared their recipes with us (noted within).

Table of Contents

Introduction
Sweet
Pepsi Rain 1
    Pepsi Brownies 4
Tie-Dyed Dress 5
    Rainbow Jell-O 8
Coconut Love 10
    Coconut Candy 13
Chocolate Therapy 15
    Easy Champulådu 16
Got Eggnog? 17
    Eggnog French Toast 18
    Epic Monte Cristo 18
A Song for Sandwich Cookies 19
    Whoopie Pies 20
Recipe for a Song 21
    Icebox Cake 23
    Trifle 24
    Turtle Cake 25
A Sticky Situation 26
    Applesauce Cake 28
Friendship Garden 29
    Dirt Cake 31
Always 33
    Spice Squares 35
Mocha Fredo 37
    Best Fudge Ever 39
Big Sister 41

Sweet Dinner Rolls	43
Little Sister	45
Sugar Cookies and Icing	47
Pistachio Cake with Almond Glaze	51
Let Them Eat Cake!	53
Black Forest Cake	55
Drunken Cakes	56
Potu	58
Crème de Menthe Cake	59
Savory	60
Marina Restaurant	61
Blue Cheese Salad	63
Sweet Pairings	64
Fondue	66
To Spam or Not to Spam	67
Seconds Pasta	69
The Magic of Cheese	71
Mac 'N Cheese	73
Hyperlexic Parenting	75
Cucumber and Soy Sauce Salad	76
For the Love of Salami	77
Caprese Denisi	79
Cousins	80
Brie en Cruste	81
One of These Things is Not Like the Other	82
Cannelloni	84
Meatloaf	86
Meatball Loaf	87
Italian Meatballs	89
Uncle Pat's Meatballs	90

Scandalous! Unpopular Opinion 91
    Roman Beans 93
    Filet Mignon & Red Wine Sauce 95
The Trouble with Chicken 96
    Lemon Chicken Pesto 98
    Savory Chicken Squares 99
    Easy Chicken Parmesan 101
    Garlic Bread 101
Teriyaki Sticks 102
    Teriyaki Marinade 103
Bacon 104
    Ferghetti and Hammer 106
Gnocchi 107
    Mashed Potato Spring Rolls with Bacon and Cheese 110
Juxtaposition Picnic 111
    Family Picnic Sandwich 113
Holy Spirit Pot Luck 114
    Spinach Casserole 117
Way Back Wednesday 118
    Salami and Cheddar Wraps 120
    Apple Butter Sandwich 121
Roast beef on ciabatta with sundried tomato ricotta pesto 122
A Faithful Friend 123
    Sautéed Cabbage with Bacon and Pecans 125
Rice, Rice, Baby 126
    Red Rice 128
Remembering Grandma Santos 129
    Titiyas 131
    Fina'denne 132
    Chicken Kelaguen 133

Simple Gifts 135
    Stuffed Mushrooms 136
Reflections 138
References: 139
For the Reader 140
About the Author 141

Introduction

How many times have had with Pepsi dumped on you? Well it's happened to me more than once! I have a one-pot pasta which I call Seconds Pasta, because. And when my hubby travels out of town, the kids and I feast upon the dishes that he doesn't enjoy. Who doesn't enjoy Fondue? Some are stories behind the dishes, some are stories about the ingredients.

I have been doused with Pepsi on more than one occasion and can tell you that the last thing you want is to take a syrupy shower in movie theater seats. How many people can say the same? And not many people can say they have a ridiculous secret for baking delicious Pepsi brownies either.

Have you ever wondered how recipes got invented? A good recipe reads kind of like a story. Think about it: It starts with an introduction with the ingredients list as its table of contents, and the beginning to end instructions are the recipe's story of how to make the meal. Whomever creates a recipe invites a future cook to participate in the story much like an author creates a narrative for a reader to interact within a book's pages. It is an invitation to read and participate in the story.

I totally dig the interactive story of a good recipe. I also like to change the ending just a bit with a surprise twist or a personal favorite and creative addition. I have altered and modified recipes to make them more appealing for children or to lessen the preparation time, or in some cases, for health concerns.

There is also part of me that thinks it is pretty absurd to write a recipe. Who am I to tell you how much cheese to add? Don't listen to me; just add more, if you want! Heck, most of the time I make a bigger meatloaf anyway, so I don't even follow my own recipe. Adjust the quantities as you see fit. And I am not going to provide calorie counts for you. Because how am I to know if you choose a calorific ingredient instead of a lean one?

One of the many invaluable lessons I learned while growing up in a multi-cultural household in such a diverse family is that there are many different ways to do something "right". As I grew older and came to learn and respect the many world faiths, I chose to purse my own faith in academics. I've always recognized, though, how hurtful it is to be judged for whatever reason, whether it was by others in my own faith or by those in graduate school who judged me for my appearance, gender, age or marital status. But you know what? All of these experiences deepened my own personal faith experience. And, all of these experiences strengthened my belief that, like recipes, there are so many so many colors and flavors in the world. We all have something unique to offer, and yet we are united in our sharing of uniqueness.

There are stories behind recipes. And there are stories stirred and folded within mine, like a ribbon of caramel in your crème brûlée. That's what I'm talking about! I share these not-so-conventional yet delicious family recipes and the stories that go along with them with you in hopes that you will enjoy them as much as I have.

Now, it's *Boka*[1] time!

---

[1] *Boka* is Chamorro for Eat/Eating

Sweet

Pepsi Rain

Strangely enough, I have found myself where Pepsi has been thrown at me, more than once. Some people are just lucky, I guess and even luckier that it's only Pepsi. My sister attracts flying objects to her head. Perhaps it is in the genes. Case in point, there were 600 people were popping champagne bottles open at my cousin's island-style wedding and my sister was the only person to be hit in the head with a flying cork.

The first time I experienced projectile Pepsi was in college. A group of friends, including my sister, and I wanted to see the movie *The Firm*, based on the book by John Grisham and starring Tom Cruise. The book flew off the shelves soon after it was published in 1991. I distinctly remember being so engrossed in reading it sitting on my bed in my college dorm, that when my dear sister hovered in the doorway speaking to me, my brain initially registered her as part of the story. (Has this happened to anybody else? Bueller?) So, I really wanted to see it when the movie came out.

We didn't have smart phones, et cetera in 1993, rather we had to find an actual printed newspaper in order to check the movie times. There was no Fandango! We actually drove to three theaters that day and found that it was sold out at each of the first two. Finally, we sat on the sidewalk near Hayward Festival Cinema for four hours waiting for the last matinee showing. Finally we get into the theater where I end up sitting at the end of the row of my friends and next to a stranger who was an older guy on my right. I'm not sure how old he was, but during that beach scene (You know the one, the one on the beach when Tom Cruise is seduced by an exotic woman on the beach.) he spazzed-out and squeezed his big gulp Pepsi. The syrupy liquid flew upward and cascaded onto me like an amber waterfall, in all of its wonderfully sticky glory.

My entire right side was drenched with sparkling syrup. The guy muttered something and scooted to the empty seat beside him. Seriously, a big creepy jerk. I had two choices: leave immediately to get cleaned up and miss the movie, or stay and watch the movie. I stayed. We had driven to three theaters in three cities and sat on the hot July sidewalk, for crying out loud.

The next time I endured a shower of Pepsi rain was in Las Vegas. I was about 27, and we were celebrating my friend's 30th birthday at the Excalibur Hotel and Casino. We were watching the jousting tournament when the announcer had just said her name and the fact that it was her birthday. She stood up and everyone applauded. We were seated stadium-style and there was a long counter in front of our seats, serving as a table.

During this lively, medieval-themed show, dinner was served during the event and included a miniature game hen, bread roll, maybe some soup, and a goblet filled with the beverage of your choice. To encourage audience participation, the announcer tells everyone to cheer, yell, stomp their feet, and bang on the counters. Again, I ended up on the end of our bunch of friends and a stranger on my right. This dude was much larger than I was and proceeded to exuberantly slam his fist onto the counter in quick succession like everybody else. This guy, however, was a bit maniacal about it.

It happened in slow motion, like an instant replay -- I couldn't do anything about. He pounded his fist too near his goblet and it rose, not straight up, of course, but straight at me because I am a magnet for Pepsi. The icy-cold, bubbly syrup doused my little black dress and me as if it had been gushing out of a fire hydrant.

This time, the dude apologized. The rest of my party was so engrossed in the jousting show that they didn't even notice all our commotion. The balding, red plaid flannel shirt guy was with his family, including a couple of young children. He politely refrained from pounding his fist for the duration of the show. My dress was ruined. But what happens in Vegas stays in Vegas, right?

Pepsi Brownies

It really is almost embarrassing, how easy this recipe is to make. My sister heard it from a stranger at a Weight Watchers meeting. We tried it at home for a family dinner, and the rest is history. As my children's dear Auntie Noel said, "It's magic."

Ingredients:

1 box of your favorite brownie mix

1 12 oz. can of your favorite soda (I like to use Cherry Pepsi)

(Nothing else! Seriously! For real. No eggs. You don't even have to butter the pan.)

Directions:

Pour the brownie mix into a large bowl.

Pour the soda. Stir until well mixed.

Pour into pan (I usually use a 9 X 12 pan)

Bake according to directions on the brownie mix box.

Most boxes give you a range—the longer side will bake through and become cake—like, the shorter baking time creates a nice syrupy brownie.

Great with vanilla ice cream!

Tie-Dyed Dress

I love arts and crafts festivals, and not for the reason you think. I love the tie-dye vendors with their tie-dye rainbow banners flags marking their booths.

Flashback to 1994: I was working at the San Jose Barnes & Noble Bookseller flagship store when I had a day shift at the bookstore's booth at an arts and crafts fair downtown, and there was no parking. I got lost trying to find our booth. They said it was "by the library," which is, of course, subjective, and not nearly detailed enough. It was also hot as Hell.

I finally arrived (late) at said booth and the gal from the previous shift took one look at me, dressed in a long-sleeved cobalt blue silk blouse, black suede pencil skirt, black suede high heels, and nylons (back when it was fashionable to wear them), and said, "Go buy something tie-dyed."

Fortunately, the tie-dyed banners floated somewhat nearby and I was able to purchase a wondrous tie-dye bright rainbow tank knee-length dress. I suppose it could have been called a shift, but it was more than likely designed as a bathing suit cover-up. Surprisingly high quality, the vibrant colors just popped like fresh paint. I think I had to find a bank or hotel with a restroom to change into the tank dress, and lose the nylons. I was stuck in my black pumps however and fortunately, I had either a big hair clip or scrunchie to pull my hair up and back. I was certainly more comfortable, though perhaps less professional. The ensemble seemed to work, in a multicultural art fair kind of way.

I was living and working in an undergraduate dorm at Santa Clara University at the time as a grad student in Pastoral

Ministry/ Liturgical Music. That summer my eleven-story dorm was being worked on for some reason and the residents had to wear hard hats to go in and out of the building. I remember wearing the tie-dye dress, walking down Market Street en route to the dorm when a car driving past honked. I decided to ignore it but it turns out it was Sister Head Nun, the director of my graduate program, and not the only nun who seemed to disapprove of me. They would ignore or patronize me in class ("Denise, you need to wear a barrette, and maybe some shoulder pads.") and yet honk, wave, and smile on campus.

The tie-dyed tank dress was crazy fun to wear; I'd bring it traveling as either a cover-up or nightgown. I vaguely recall changing out of my Pretty Woman-style white polka dot dress in the car after Mass into the magic tie-dyed dress for a day at the Great America Amusement Park. From the belted long rayon dress and heels to the tie-dyed loose shift and sandals, wahoo! (Let the people say, Amen!)

A year or two later, happily employed as a church music director, I traveled to the annual national music directors' convention in Denver (yes, there really is such an event) but the hotel closest to the convention was overbooked so I had to stay in one farther away. I had to get up extra early to take a taxi to the convention, and wouldn't you know it, I had left the tie-dyed dress on the hook behind the bathroom door in the hotel room. I remember calling Lost and Found later, describing my wonderful dress, thinking that I'd never get it back. The woman on the phone seemed very interested in my dress. And really, who wouldn't? I never got it back. I was sad, but not surprised.

Two years later, I was at another arts and craft fair. I saw the striking tie-dyed banners in the pattern of my dress. And to my great delight, it was the same vendor who had sold me my fabulous tie-dyed tank dress. She was selling the same dress! I snapped one up. I still have the dress, though there seems to be fewer occasions to sport a tie-dyed dress. I simply cannot part with it however.

At yet another arts and craft fair nearly ten years later I found the same tie-dye vendor. I was with my then-18 month-old son and our playgroup. She had the awesome sunburst rainbow tie- dyed design in kids' shirts. So of course, I had to get one for my son. He wore it in his kindergarten photo and he is also wearing it in a photo I put in my daughter's birth brag book. When he began to outgrow it, I had him wear it in a professional photo session to immortalize it.

Once when my daughter was a toddler, I searched for a shirt for her to wear to preschool. I gave her a choice: a white shirt with a rainbow on it or her brother's rainbow tie-dyed shirt which he had outgrown. Her eyes lit up and she confidently planted her sweet little hand on the tie-dyed shirt. Delighted, I paired it with some crazy white polka-dotted light green leggings. She received so many compliments at school. With her fair skin and black hair, the colors just pop. I must say, she wore it well. And she told all her friends and teachers it was "Wainbow tie-dye."

Someday I'll give her my tie-dyed tank dress. And tell her this story.

Rainbow Jell-O

A favorite snack that my mother made for us kids many times when we were young. And now that I see how much love goes in to preparing it, I adore it even more. "Time and patience," my mother always says.

Ingredients:

6 small packages flavored gelatin (3 oz.) (Grape, Blue raspberry, Lime, Lemon, Orange, Cherry)

4 packages Knox unflavored gelatin

1 14 oz. can Sweetened condensed milk

Glass 9x13 pan

Directions:

First layer: Mix 1 package any flavor gelatin with 1 teaspoon Knox gelatin and 1 cup boiling water. Cool and pour into glass casserole dish. Refrigerate until set, about 30 minutes. While waiting, start boiling the next layer.

Second layer: mix one envelope Knox gelatin with ½ cup hot water until it dissolves. Add ½ can condensed milk and an additional ½ cup hot water. Once this is cool, pour ¾ cup of this concoction on top of the firm gelatin. Chill for 30 minutes. Immediately start making the next color layer

Repeat steps one and two (using the rest of the while mix ¾ cup at a time for the thin layer) ending with a colored gelatin on top.

Halfway through this process you will need to make the second half of your white mixture. Don't do it all at once or it will gel in your mixing bowl. Once you run out of white mixture, mix one envelope Knox gelatin with ½ cup hot water until it dissolves. Add ½ can condensed milk and an additional ½ cup hot water. Once this is cool, pour ¾ cup of this concoction on top of the firm gelatin.

Once finished, cover with plastic wrap and refrigerate overnight to set good. Before serving, slice into rectangles!

I recommend starting with a purple on the bottom. Then blue, green, yellow, orange and red. There will be white layers in between each color, with the red on top. You can also vary the colors to match your school colors, team colors, or holiday colors.

Coconut Love

Have you ever enjoyed the sweet milk of a fresh coconut? Or had freshly grated coconut? Then this story is for you.

My husband and I both enjoyed coconut when we were kids. My husband's family is of Italian and Irish Jewish descent and are from New York. They moved to Southern California in the early 1970's, then to Silicon Valley, Northern California. My husband tells us stories of how he and his younger sister used to watch their father battle a coconut to open it. Lots of garage tools were involved, apparently. The kids watched and waited for a long time. The proper method of opening a coconut seemed to be – simply getting mad at it.

Meanwhile, I grew up thirty miles north, with an Irish San Franciscan father and a Chamorro/ Guamanian mother. (Where is Guam, anyway? Guam is a tiny island territory three hours east of Japan, the southernmost island in the Northern Marianas Islands.) She had a coconut-opening tool called a kåmyu, a staple in Chamorro Guamanian households. It never occurred to me that other families might not have heard of such a thing. (I had to do some research on this and discovered that they were banned in the United States.)

The kåmyu resembles a small bench with tools protruding from the end(s). You straddle the bench and place a bowl beneath the grater. It has an ice pick on one end for piercing the coconut. You let the milk fall into the bowl below. Then using the six-pronged grating tool affixed to the end of the bench, you hold the coconut halves upside down and systematically scrape the insides out. The meat of the coconut falls into the bowl below- like snow. Chamorro people, young and old, do this. Nowadays you can buy smaller devices that are more like a cutting board with the grating tool on the end but the method is still the same. You can find tons of videos on YouTube demonstrating the products.

Recently my family had the opportunity to visit my mother's island of Guam. I've traveled there before with my parents and then with my husband, but this was before we had children. This recent trip was special as it was our kids' first visit. When our Guamanian Chamorro family greeted us, they said warmly, "Welcome Home."

We were so lucky to enjoy several family barbeque meals, which is exactly what family meals are all about: Cherished family time! We are all family, with first cousins and even fourth cousins far removed. It was wonderful hearing the traditional blessing spoken in the native language, led by my cousin's children. There were easily fifty people assembled for us on a Tuesday evening! Of course, they insisted, "No, this is not a party, this is just a barbeque!"

The next evening we visited Chamorro Village, a modern structure which houses an outdoor food and art festival every Wednesday. There are food vendors, artist booths, animals to visit, music and dancing. ATMs are driven to the curb in trailers, and the tourists line up to get cash for the food booths and artisans. In the main hall, my young daughter and I joined the line dancers for the Cha Cha Slide.

We were delighted to find sugar-coated fried banana doughnuts on a skewer, fresh coconut, marinated beef, and so much more!

We poked straws into a green coconut and drank its milk, straight from the fruit.

We also visited the Lina'la' Chamorro Culture Park, a recreation of a pre-Magellan Chamorro village life 500 years ago. The immersion into the culture is a fantastic journey. There are movies and artifacts, a nature walk, and the village's structures, which stand over an actual Chamorro village site. A young man girded in only a loincloth guided us through the village structures and opened a coconut for the six of us. The fresh coconut meat is so delicious sweet and tender, it makes prepackaged coconut flakes taste like a cheap facsimile. I swear, the milk is magic.

Coconut Candy

Once my mother learned that I had a college class with another Guamanian girl, she made this candy especially for her. That is the kind of person my mom is. She knows it is hard to be away from your homeland, especially when it is such a glorious island.

There was a woman in the parish when I was a church choir director who said my mother resembled her own mother who had passed away long ago. I brought my mom to meet the woman, and Mom gave her a big, warm, embrace, and said, "From Your Mother." How beautiful is that? What a gift.

Here is the coconut candy recipe, from my mother.

Ingredients:

2 large coconuts

2 cups white, granulated sugar

Directions:

Finely grate the coconut. They have to be as small as possible. This makes a difference. You should end up with 4 cups of grated coconut. If you are using prepackaged coconut, please make sure it is the UN-sweetened kind!

Caramelize the sugar in a large frying pan over low heat. Once the sugar starts melting, use a spoon or heat-safe spatula to push the sugar from the edge of the pan to the middle. It will clump, but do not worry. When it is a lush caramel color, smash the remaining clumps.

Add the coconut. The sugar will harden again, but do not worry. It is not pretty at this point. Stir and mix, and the sugar will melt again.

Turn off the heat, and form the candy in tablespoon dollops, placing on wax paper. You can roll them into balls. But I remember just the little mounds of coconut. You can wrap them in plastic to last about two weeks, but who are you kidding? It will be all eaten up way before then!

Chocolate Therapy

Have you ever felt so alone that nobody understood? Or worse, that nobody cared? My friends, I just want to tell you that I have been there. And it gets better. It does.

I have been miserable. I have had my kidney suddenly stop working properly. I have had recurring gallbladder attacks -- worse than labor -- for nearly a year before I had the darn thing taken out. I have felt betrayed by my body.

I've also felt miserably alone. When your first child isn't speaking and no other parent really understands (even if they say that they do). When your child is diagnosed as being on the Autism Spectrum, and again, no one really understands that. (Or so it seems.) I felt betrayed by my friends.

I have high functioning anxiety. I now know that my anxiety may be based on logical fear, however spiraling out of my creative imagination. One way of coping with anxiety is by turning it all off and going numb and into depression. I've felt betrayed by my own mind.

But here's the thing: Just when I think that absolutely no one understands, somebody says, "Me, too."

I now have a toolkit of wellness practices in my never-ending quest for balance. I am discovering that it is a quest and a journey, not a destination. And so, I keep journeying toward the light.

One of my ways to keep the anxiety away is by being creative. I write, read, blog, and play music. I love to craft and cook.

Sometimes the only way is a little chocolate therapy.

Am I right?

Easy Champulådu

This is sweet dessert, which is basically a chocolate rice pudding. There are many ways to prepare champulådu: over a stove, double boiler for melting chocolate, etc. This microwave way is so easy—I've made a single serving at work! I vaguely recall enjoying this as a child. My cousin reminded me of this when we visited her home in Guam in 2001. It can be served hot or cold. Cousin Sandra says, "It's good for rainy days."

Ingredients:

2 cups cooked rice

1 envelope instant hot cocoa

milk (about 1 cup)

Directions:

Heat up the rice.

Add cocoa powder.

Add milk.

Stir.

Serve and enjoy!

Got Eggnog?

Something I look forward to every year is my Eggnog French Toast. I invented this one holiday season while I was looking for ways to finish eggnog. (I should have submitted this in Rachael Ray's contest! I KNOW!) My family loves it; even the kids do! Now they think regular French toast is boring. The eggnog does make it rich, and kind of soft, so you can cut it with a fork. The real maple syrup enhances the flavor of the eggnog; I swear you can taste the nutmeg, even though we don't add any. It's like Crème Brûlée! Now I make it for Christmas brunch.

One of my favorite memories is the first time Dear Son tried eggnog when he was 13 months old. We were at my sister's first home the week before Christmas, which is when both my parents and I have our birthdays. He drank almost the entire sippy cup in one long, drawn gulp. And burped.

Eggnog French Toast

Ingredients:

    3 eggs

    1 cup eggnog

    Thick sourdough bread

    Real maple syrup

    Butter or cooking spray for pan

Directions:

    Crack eggs in a wide bowl.

    Stir in eggnog.

    Coat sourdough bread slices, wiping off excess egg batter.

    Cook both sides.

    Serve with real maple syrup.

Epic Monte Cristo

Directions:

    Right before the last sides of the French toast are done, place a slice of ham and a slice of cheese in between the "done" sides, and continue like it's a grilled cheese sandwich. The eggnog makes it heavenly!

A Song for Sandwich Cookies

Growing up as an Introverted Intuitive Feeling Perceiver (on the Myers Briggs Type Indicator MBTI-- look it up), I eschewed structure to a certain extent. I had confidence in following my heart, even going against the grain. You could say I was a different drum. I had my electronic keyboard placed atop the dorm desk, and never used the desk as it was intended.

But I also have a certain level of respect for structure, even though it is the opposite of my true nature. I did marry an engineer, an Introverted Sensing Thinking "Judging" type. I guess it is true that opposite attract.

I remember figuring out the algorithm that was the college catalog. I determined when the finite math and science of heredity courses were offered and counseled my liberal arts friends on schedule planning. I was also composing a lot of music during this time, and came to respect patterns.

Contemporary popular music and liturgical music share a lot in common. Western music has its own flavors, ingredients and recipes. A basic pattern found in both is verse-refrain. Sometimes there is a bridge section, distinctly different from the verse and refrain, but essential to the development of the song.

When I think of sandwich cookies, I think of the structure of a song, or a story. More than beginning, middle, and end, it is more like chorus, verse, and chorus. The verse in the middle is like the crème filling. But the chocolate choruses hold it all together. Music for the taste buds.

Whoopie Pies

Ingredients:

For the Cookie

    1 cup sugar

    ⅓ cup shortening

    1 egg (whole)

    1 cup milk

    1 teaspoon vanilla

    2 cups flour

    1½ teaspoons baking soda

    1 teaspoon salt

    7 tablespoons cocoa

For the Filling

    ½ cup shortening

    2 cups powdered sugar

    1 teaspoon vanilla

Directions:

Preheat oven to 425° F

Mix sugar, shortening, egg, milk, vanilla, baking soda, salt, and cocoa together. Drop by teaspoons full on ungreased cookie sheet. Bake for five to eight minutes.

For the filling, beat all ingredients together with electric mixer until fluffy. Spread filling between two cooled cookies. Enjoy!

Recipe for a Song

As a trained musician, I possess the questionable fortune of detecting musical structure whenever I hear a song. I am not even consciously trying to pick up on it, I just hear a song and I understand how it is put together. You might not know exactly what this is like, but I bet you have some music identification ability, yourself. For example, when you turn on the radio, you can tell if it is on a Country station or not. This is music style identification. There you go. You can identify if it's a song that you like. You may even know the words. You might even know when the guitar solo starts. You probably can identify the chorus. Right?

I love music of many styles and eras. I love to hear how some compositions evoke the style of another composer's work. It is an honor that they have done this. It's not copying. Contemporary piano composer Brian Crain's piece "Reminiscence" is reminiscent of the French composer Erik Satie's pieces "Gymnopedie" and "Gnossiene." Unfortunately, there does exist some blaring plagiarism in the music industry, as well. But as a composer, I can tell you -- you may not remember what other music, art, and life experience has influenced you to write that composition, sometimes not until years after the fact.

Western music has only twelve notes. But really, there are only eight when you are talking about popular music, which is written in a major (or minor) key, using an 8-note scale. Without getting too technical, there are only so many chords, and a kind of musical gravity dictates that certain chords are used more than others.

My point is, the list of available ingredients is finite.

Is it any wonder, then, that songs composed years apart and recorded by different artists for different purposes may have similar melodies and chord progressions?

Sheet music and chord charts are what musicians read to play music. They are like recipes for the songs. A lot of recipes are similar. You can search online for Brazilian Cheese Balls and find hundreds of recipes. But they will be basically the same; otherwise, it would be a different recipe. Are you with me? I can search for sheet music for the song "Lean On Me," and find hundreds of versions, in any key, some with guitar chord symbols, some without, some based on the 80's recording by Club Nouveau, or some based on the 70's recording by Bill Withers. But it's all the same song.

If I want to jam with my kids, we might choose an easy version. I know the first time I learned to play excerpts from Tchaikovsky's *Nutcracker Suite*, they were simplified versions, probably published by Hal Leonard. (I still remember the light pink booklet. Anyone?) I thought I was so cool. When I was nine. The first time I played Schubert's Ave Maria at church, you can bet it was an easy version. Would I play it now? No way.

I gave a recital a few years ago, and decided to perform "The Prayer", composed by David Foster. My duet partner and I had several decisions to make -- which version we would sing, in what key, and were we going to sing the bridge section in Italian or not? I have always considered myself to be an alto, despite my higher speaking voice, and therefore I thought we would perform the Celine Dion version, which contained some lovely low notes. As it turns out, I was feeling more like a soprano, so we performed the Charlotte Church version, with fewer low notes.

When I think about recipes, I think about how there are so many versions of a song. So many ways to tell the same story.

So many ways to make a trifle. It's all good.

Icebox Cake

This is an easy, old recipe -- a favorite of my husband's. I can just imagine people creating little icebox cakes and placing them in the old-fashioned refrigerators with blocks of ice atop, delighting children everywhere. I love this recipe because it is really a trifle.

Ingredients:

    Graham crackers

    Cool whip whipped topping

    Chocolate pudding

    Milk for the pudding

Directions:

    In a glass meatloaf pan, layer the graham crackers and chocolate pudding. Refrigerate.

    Serve with cool whip whipped topping on top.

Trifle

Ingredients:

- Pound cake
- Jam
- Sherry or simple syrup
- Prepared vanilla pudding
- Whipped cream or whipped topping
- You need a tall glass bowl for this.

Directions:

Slice the cake into cubes, cover the bottom of the bowl.

Drizzle with sherry, or if you will be serving to children, use simple syrup (equal parts sugar and water).

Cover cake pieces with fruit jam. Cover jam layer with vanilla pudding. Repeat until glass bowl is almost full.

Top with whipped cream or whipped topping.

Turtle Cake

This is based on the famous turtle candies, which are chocolate covered caramels that resemble turtle-looking discs.

Ingredients:

- 1 package chocolate cake mix
- 1 pound caramels (about 54 pieces)
- 1 can evaporated milk
- 1 package of chocolate chips
- 1 cup nuts
- eggs, oil, water, according to the box mix

Directions:

Preheat oven to 350°.

Mix according to the directions on the box

Pour half of the batter mixture into a 9 x 13, greased and floured baking pan.

Bake for about 10 minutes until almost set. Remove from oven.

While it cools, melt caramels and pour in evaporated milk.

Pour mixture over partially baked cake.

Sprinkle in chocolate chips and nuts.

Pour remaining chocolate batter over the top of the baked mixture and continue baking an additional 25-30 minutes more. Cool and frost or just sprinkle with powdered sugar.

A Sticky Situation

My sweet young baby boy loved his applesauce when he was a baby. I often would blend cooked carrots into his applesauce, at home. Nana would make him applesauce from scratch. After trick-or-treating, he proudly counted his shiny wrapped candy bars, and then requested applesauce. Normally, applesauce is not a bad thing! But, we once experienced quite a sticky situation involving applesauce. Whenever I hear Def Leppard's song "Pour Some Sugar on Me" this is what comes to mind.

My Dear Son was a man of few words when he was a toddler. We had started calling him Mellow Man. He was extraordinarily well-behaved, though, and a delight to take to restaurants. Yeah I know; this is rare.

On this particular day in the Adventures of Mellow Man, I brought him to lunch with our dear friend, his Auntie Rachel. Although she's not related, she grew up with my husband and she's the one who set us up, so we call her family. We were dining at Bennigan's, a delightful American restaurant chain with tchotchkes on the walls. Like every other American restaurant chain, right? This one has some pretty special broccoli bites or something, as I recall. These were broccoli, cheese, and bacon, battered, and deep-fried. (Right? I know, my arteries just got scared, too.)

The two-year-old was seated happily in a wooden high chair, pulled up to the table. We enjoyed lunch and conversation, laughing as we do whenever we get together. We were reminiscing about some of the fun we've had together, like the time we went to all the Burger Kings in South San Jose for "Free Fries Day." And the time she screwed up the words in the Alleluia verse so badly, she voluntarily removed herself from the cantor podium with an imaginary hook and cane. Or my wedding video, in which everyone else in the wedding party said *"Thank you for choosing me to be in your special day..."* and she said, "You're welcome." I hope everybody has a special friend like this.

I had ordered apples instead of fries for his kiddie meal—as apples are healthier, right? They came in a heated bowl with raisins and sugar—it was more like pie filling. I took out the apple slices, diced them some more, placed them on a clean bread plate for my son, and gave him a spoon. He seemed content, and we gals continued talking and digging into to our lava cake.

Suddenly, I look over at my son, who is visibly discontent as he is trying to wipe off the gooey apples from his hands. Quite unsuccessfully, I might add. In fact, in his attempts to wipe the goo off, he inadvertently had wiped sticky sugary apple-y goo all over his hands, and up and down his arms, as well.

"Oh, My God!" I exclaimed. And then, to Rachel, "Can you grab an arm?"

Rachel says he was all oiled up like a pro-wrestler. (I don't watch wrestling, so, whatever.) Seriously, he was glistening. It took each of us two pre-moistened wipes and two napkins to erase away the goo. Then we had to wrestle him out of the high chair and to the bathroom sink. We were laughing hysterically as Auntie Rachel held the toddler in front of her at arms' length while he, in turn, held his arms out in front of him, like a little Frankenstein. We managed to get him to the bathroom sink and she balanced the boy between herself and the sink, while I scrubbed his little hands and arms with soap.

Pour some sugar on me.

Applesauce Cake

This is one of my favorites of my mom's recipes. It's delightfully sweet and unique.

Ingredients:

    2 cups flour

    1 ¼ cups sugar

    1 tablespoon corn starch

    2 tablespoons cocoa

    2 teaspoon baking soda

    ½ teaspoon salt (optional)

    ½ teaspoon cinnamon

    ½ teaspoon nutmeg

    1 ½ cups Applesauce

    1 cup raisins (soaked in warm water and drained)

    ½ cup oil

    1 cup chopped walnuts (optional)

Directions:

    Dump dry ingredients into a large bowl.

    Add one at a time without mixing, applesauce, raisins, oil and walnuts.

    Mix well, then pour into well-greased angel food or 13x9 pan

    Bake in 350 oven for 40 to 50 minutes. Test with toothpick for doneness.

    (Cupcakes: only 20-25 mins)

Friendship Garden

As you approach the front door of my parents' home, you will note a sweet, wild garden to the left, under the dining room window. My sweet mother saves roses and flowers from loved one's funerals, receptions, and plants them in this flower bed. As the flowers bloom in season, we remember our dear friends who have gone before us.

Mom included roses from our friend Hilary. My sister and I were so lucky to meet and befriend this beautiful spirit when we were in college. She was beautiful and remarkable, funny and sweet. Hilary used a motorized wheelchair and my sister would often help carry her food tray at the cafeteria. Soon she became her most trusted friend.

Hilary lived happily among friends, despite the Muscular Dystrophy that had invaded her body. We learned so much from Hilary -- including how to get around challenges, often those we had previously taken for granted. And yet, we had so much fun taking her to Southern California and Mexico. We went to see the musical *Les Miserables* in San Francisco, and enjoyed a fabulous adventure getting there and back. Hilary also visited Lake Tahoe and Yosemite. She was part of our college education -- we learned perspective, humility, helpfulness, gratitude and happiness.

I believe Hilary was an angel sent to inspire us. She had a unique ability to bring out the good in other people. Sure, her friends helped her get around. But she helped us, too.

The years after graduation were hard. Her muscular degeneration had accelerated and you could hear it in her voice. Her friends had moved and she had minimal support in independent living. Still she was able to visit schools and inspire children. It breaks my heart that she suffered so much, and died at the tender age of twenty-three.

Hilary's roses are now in full bloom: a pink and yellow hybrid with a peachy glow. I let myself in the front door, and my mother called to me, with a smile in her voice, "Did you see Hilary?"

Yes, I did. It's like Hilary is sending us a message from the other side. She's alright. And she can move around.

You can read about Hilary in her own words.

http://www.theinsite.org/been_there/fr_auto_jus.html

http://www.theinsite.org/been_there/hilary_phys_dis.html

Dirt Cake

This is such a fun dessert. It's tasty and all about the presentation. My mother used to serve it in a foil lined terra cotta flower pot. You can even buy a trowel but only use it for this recipe. No actual gardening! I have even found a Pyrex bowl covered in terra cotta! This recipe is so much fun for the kids (even the big kids)!

Needed:

1 clean flower pot

1 clean shovel

Ingredients:

2 small boxes vanilla pudding

milk for pudding (as described on box)

1 cup powdered sugar

1 lb. Oreo cookies (42 cookies, the regular kind. "Double stuffed" gets too sticky.)

8 oz. cool whip

1 brick cream cheese, softened

Directions:

Put the cookies in a zip-lock baggie and let the kids hammer away. (Sometimes it's really good for me to let out a little aggression, too, with a meat tenderizer and those 42 cookies in a large pasta pot.) I have tried using food processors but the blades often get stuck, which is annoying.

Mix softened cream cheese and powdered sugar with fork.

In separate bowl, mix pudding and milk. Add cool whip, mix. Add contents of first bowl and mix.

Alternate layers of pudding and cookie crumbs in flower pot as desired. Be sure to leave enough crumbs for the top layer.

Refrigerate overnight (I KNOW, THIS PART IS ALWAYS SO HARD!) Or at least one hour before serving. You can handle at least that, right? Right? Step away from the refrigerator!

Display with shovel for serving.

*For garnish, add strawberries, fake flowers, or gummy worms.

*Or, for Irish Dirt Cake: add 1 teaspoon mint extract and a few drops of green food coloring.

Always

Whenever I fly, I enjoy a glass of ginger ale. It takes me back to when I was child. We would often take the hour-long journey across the Bay Bridge to Grandma and Grandpa's house in San Francisco. They would welcome us with ginger ale and goldfish crackers (parmesan or original). As I described this memory to my husband on the plane, I nearly cried.

Such a tender collection of memories, and even just thinking about it, I can taste the sensation of the salty, cheesy crackers and feel the rough of the cracker edges on my tongue, accompanied by swirls of bubbly ginger ale.

And I remember the sweet love from my dear grandparents. I cannot isolate just one memory, there are too many of them. The old yellow carpet. The new mint curtains. Aunt Marie's old bedroom in the back. The paper guest towels on the towel rack in the upstairs bathroom Grandma put out for us. The smell of sweet tobacco from Grandpa's pipe..

Every Christmas Eve, we ate downstairs in the basement with my sister and our 16 cousins. Grandpa counted the meatballs in Grandma's lasagna. We would have creamed spinach in white sauce, fruit cocktail gelatin with "dressing" (fruit juice and mayonnaise), and chocolate cream pie. After dinner, the adults came down and we all opened the kids' gifts. Then we played with the toys all over the house while the adults exchanged gifts upstairs. The girl cousins played with Sindy dolls and accessories in the first bedroom upstairs. The closet chronicled their six children and all 18 grandchildren's heights measured at various dates. "Always" by Irving Berlin was their song, and the sheet music was lovingly framed and displayed above their "modern" 70's eight-track/ cassette/ record player stereo combo unit.

As a young adult, I gravitated more to visiting the closet of grandpa's meticulously chronicled and labeled photo albums, scrapbook style. We are so lucky he did this. We are aware of our family history. He gave us a great gift. My own father has inherited those albums. Needless to say, they are precious treasures.

I hope my son remembers the wonderful times he has at my own parents' house: that three o' clock is "yogurt time" or maybe a cream cheese with pineapple sandwich on raisin bread will someday take him back to memories of Nana and Papa's place.

So, whenever I happen to be drinking ginger ale, I raise a glass to Grandma and Grandpa.

Spice Squares

My mom learned this delightful recipe from my paternal grandmother, who got it from her mother-in-law. My four Irish aunts and my mother seem to make it slightly differently, and that is part of the fun, just like when they make their tortilla casseroles and Irish soda bread. You have to taste each one offered. For me, I prefer the way my own mother prepared it. The difference is in the condensed milk. That's where the magic happens. So many modern recipes have conveniences and tricks, and if you are reading this book then you know I love timesaving tricks. But I also love to take the time to follow an old recipe the right way, with all the spices and no prepared mixes. From scratch.

Ingredients:

For squares

    3 eggs

    1 cup sugar

    1 cup flour

    3 tablespoons cocoa

    1 teaspoon powder

    3 tablespoons water

    ½ teaspoon cinnamon

    ½ teaspoon nutmeg

    ½ teaspoon cloves

For frosting

    ½ cube butter or margarine

    10 tablespoon. sifted powdered sugar

3 tablespoon. cream or evaporated milk

3 tablespoon. cocoa

Directions:

For squares:

Preheat oven to 350°

Combine eggs and sugar and beat well. Add flour, cocoa, baking powder, water, cinnamon, nutmeg and cloves. Beat until well blended. Bake for 20 to 30 minutes in a two-quart baking dish.

Frosting:

Melt butter in saucepan. Add per ingredients: mix well. Return to stove and bring to a boil. Pour on cake while hot.

Mocha Fredo

I recently found out that an old friend of mine is also a mutual friend with another friend on Facebook. And the first thing she said to me was that I was a Mocha Fredo Genius. I literally laughed out loud as I remembered the times I whipped up my "famous" mochas in our college dorm.

My "recipe" was laughably easy, but everybody loved it. I made instant coffee from the Suisse Mocha Internationals line, which came in a Spam-shaped tin. And then I added a generous scoop of ice cream. I used French Silk. Seriously, that's it. But twenty years later, my sweet friend remembers.

I had a crush on a boy during my senior year in college. It wasn't a serious crush, more of an interest. I had fended off some pseudo-suitable suitors in my day (more stories); I approached this tall and handsome, unassuming boy with sandy blond hair that was overlong on top and parted to one side like an 80's boy band lead singer. He actually seemed scared when I suggested that he come to my dorm room where I could make him a mocha. (I wonder if he thought I meant something else…)

Then in grad school, where I was the pretty much the youngest student by a generation, I happened to bring the mocha makings to evening class break. I called it recess, but the nuns didn't like that. (They also mandated that I take a certain required course, even though I had just taken Christology as an undergrad, where my then-professor had literally written the course book the grad school class was now using!) They commented loudly on how no one had ever brought ice cream to evening class break before! (Seriously, did no one have fun until I got there?) But they did seem to rather enjoy my Dirt Cake, so, whatever.

Nowadays, I make my mocha fredo like this:

Caramel Cappuccino k-cup.

Two scoops ice cream.

Blend.

Because really, I believe that chocolate should be fun. And easy. Like my fudge recipe.

Best Fudge Ever

From my friend Jennifer's "Grandma B."

Note: This is an old recipe so the wattage is approximately 700-900 watts. If you have a higher wattage microwave, adjust to Medium, accordingly.

Ingredients:

¾ cup Butter (1 ½ sticks)

3 cups Sugar

2/3 cup Evaporated Milk

1 bag Chocolate Chips (11.5 oz.)

1 jar Jet-Puffed Marshmallow Crème

1 teaspoon Vanilla

Directions:

1. Butter 13 x 9 x 2 pan
2. Melt butter in large microwaveable bowl
3. Add sugar and milk
4. Microwave on High for 3 minutes
5. Stir, Microwave 2 minutes
6. Mix and Scrape, Microwave 3 minutes
7. Stir, Microwave 2 ½ minutes more
8. Stir in Chocolate Chips
9. Mix in Marshmallow and Vanilla
10. Pour in pan, cool

*Optional: Add Raspberry Extract or Almond Extract

*OR add 4 teaspoons of Cherry Syrup (from a jar of maraschino cherries)

Big Sister

My mom was the baby of seven children. She was born during World War II when the island of Guam was captured by Japan. The Chamorro people were brutally treated by the Japanese. Shortly after my mother's birth, the family was forced to march, along with other villagers, to another location. Mom's eldest sister, Doris, was nine at the time, and she was charged with carrying the newborn during the march. Doris told me later that her arm had frozen stuck into the carrying position; such was her love for her sister and the acceptance of responsibility for her care.

Doris would later become the proud owner of a bar on Marine Drive. After their father had left, she would help provide support for the large family in this way. Doris's daughter was close in age to my mother, and they shared a special bond growing up. Sadly, my Aunt Doris is no longer living. I recently visited the café that is now at the site where Doris's Place was. As my family sipped our frozen café drinks on the enclosed back porch beneath palm trees and gazed over the blue water, a glorious double rainbow appeared in the North sky. I like to think it was a gift from Doris.

I'm not sure exactly why, but we called her "Auntie Ling." I remember visiting Auntie Ling's home when I was a young girl. She would invite us in to see the bread she was baking. There were so many deep pans of bread set to rise, carefully placed all over the darkened guest room, simulating a warm oven. Each pan was covered with a kitchen towel. Auntie Ling would invite my young sister and I into the room, holding her finger in front of her lips in the "Sssh!" position with a wink, whispering and pulling back a towel to reveal the bread rising. It was kind of like a sacred shrine of the rising bread.

She (along with my other aunties) exemplifies warm, loving kindness. Despite hardships, she was always smiling, loving, and laughing. Just two of them together in the kitchen sounds like a party of twenty people! I remember Auntie Ling saying quite confidently and comically, "None of that is mine," whenever somebody else was crazy-making.

That's really profound! I often let the crazy-making of others affect my state of being. You probably have heard the saying: "Not my circus, not my monkeys." This is the same thing, only more meditative. It's hard to truly release the crazy-making circus monkeys when you are identifying them as such. Am I right?

So I started deep breathing and reciting in my mind: None of that is mine. None of that is mine. Then, I switched my breathing so I would inhale with that the words *"is Mine"* and exhale the words *"None of that..."* This is a little harder to do, and you have to concentrate to get it right. But it is so worth it in my experience. I can physically release the breath this way and psychically release the crazy-making at the same time. It's my new meditative mindfulness mantra.

Thanks, Auntie Ling!

Sweet Dinner Rolls

By Grandma Santos and Auntie Doris

Ingredients:

2 Packages Yeast

5 lbs. flour

2 eggs

1 Cup Water

2/3 cup Crisco vegetable oil

1 ½ cup Sugar

Dash Salt

4 Cups Warm Milk

Directions:

In a large bowl, combine 2 packages yeast, 1 Tablespoon sugar and 1 cup hot tap water. Let stand about ten minutes or until foamy and doubled in size.

Add a dash of salt and 4 cups of warm milk to the yeast mixture.

Whip ½ cup sugar, 2/3 cup Crisco and two eggs, then add this to milk mixture.

Add flour and stir to mix.

Dough will still be extremely sticky. Coat your hands with Crisco or butter and knead to form a ball.

Place on floured breadboard and knead about ten minutes or until the dough becomes elastic. Add flour as needed, the dough should not be sticky.

Place the dough in a large greased bowl, turning to coat.

Cover and let rise until doubled, about thirty minutes in warm oven. Punch down dough.

Divide for desired size pans, filling the pans half full. Cover and let rise until doubled in size.

Bake at 350° for 30 to 45 minutes or until golden brown.

Brush with butter or margarine or glaze with a sugar and water mixture.

Little Sister

My sister Debbie is undeniably creative and talented: she is quite the baker and cake decorator, the "Hostess with the Most-ess," if you will, and more. I was delighted when she started blogging. She's so generous -- now you can learn how she bakes her fantabulous and delicious cakes, and many of her other crafty creations, which mostly coincide with holiday decorating, visiting Disneyland in style, and throwing marvelous and grandly themed birthday parties. She's created a grand piano out of fondant for my birthday and a Harry Potter book for my son's birthday, just to start. Her parties are often featured on the website Catch My Party.

Now you can read about how she and her friends drive down to Los Angeles almost every year to catch the Red Carpet at the Emmy's -- often talking with television celebrities! Seriously, she chats it up with famous people! And then sometimes they get on TV. How lucky is she?

Debbie's philosophy of "crazy"-- is everyone's a little bit "crazy," some just let it show more than others. If your "crazy" is showing too much, just tuck it back in.

Last year she began a journey with the KonMari method of organization according to Marie Kondo's book *The Life-Changing Magic of Tidying Up: The Method of Decluttering and Organizing*. Deb has documented her reading and realizations and photographed her process on what she calls her glutton-free journey. (She what she did there?)

I am so proud of my sister and her achievements. She is so talented and generous, and I have learned so much from her! I hope you stop on by at her website Is my Crazy Showing and say hello! You can also follow IsMyCrazyShowing? On Pinterest and on Facebook.

Sugar Cookies and Icing

My sister got this recipe from a friend, who got it from a friend, who got it from Who-Knows-Where. I think it is a pretty basic recipe, similar to most sugar cookie recipes. Not all sugar cookies are created equal – sometimes they look beautiful but taste awful. I like this recipe because it is not only easy, but the cookies are super yummy. She and her girlfriends get together a few times a year to decorate cookies. They bring their own cookies and a batch or two of icing in an assigned color to share with the group. She makes her cookies ahead of time and then freezes them. You have to let them dry COMPLETELY (at least 24 hours), stack a couple, wrap them in plastic wrap, then aluminum foil, and place them in a sealed container in the freezer. Take them out to defrost the day before.

This recipe makes about 60 medium-sized cookies.

Ingredients:

Cookies

    6 cups flour

    3 teaspoons baking powder

    2 cups butter

    2 cups sugar

    2 eggs

    2 teaspoons vanilla extract (vanilla bean paste) or desired flavoring (LorAnn's Almond Emulsion)

    1 teaspoon Salt

Directions:

    Preheat oven to 350° for at least a half hour before baking

cookies.

Cream butter and sugar until light and fluffy.

Add eggs and vanilla/extract.

Mix well.

Mix dry ingredients separately and add a little at a time to butter mixture.

Mix until flour is completely incorporated and the dough comes together.

Divide dough into about 6 balls.

Roll each ball in between 2 sheets of parchment paper. Roll it out to the desired thickness (quarter inch) and then place the dough and paper on a cookie sheet or cutting board and leave it in the refrigerator. Continue rolling out the rest of the dough balls between sheets of paper until you have rolled them all. By the time you are finished, the first batch should be chilled enough to cut. Re-roll leftover dough and repeat the process. I usually do this the day before and let the dough chill overnight.

CHILL dough for at least an hour. The key to the cookie not spreading is that the dough needs to be chilled and stay chilled when you pop it in the oven.

Cut into desired shape.

Bake on un-greased baking sheet at 350°F for 8 to 10 minutes or until just beginning to turn brown around the edges. Use parchment paper sheets to line the cookie sheet so it is an easy clean up and you can keep using the same cookie sheets if you have a large batch to make. Thick cookies (about a half inch thick) look very nice and professional but take a little longer to bake.

Ingredients:

Royal Icing

4 cups powdered sugar

3 tablespoons meringue powder

½ teaspoon almond extract (LorAnn's Almond Emulsion)

½ cup warm water (Don't add it all at once so you can control the consistency of the icing.)

Directions :

Combine powdered sugar, meringue powder, and extract. It is important to measure these ingredients accurately because if you use too much water or too little meringue powder, then the icing will not harden.

Add about half of the water and mix.

Add a little water at a time until it is the right consistency. Make a thick icing for the outline and then a thinner icing of the same color for the filling/inside the shape. The trick to the thickness is scooping up a spoonful of icing and then plopping it back into the bowl. Count until the icing is completely flush/re-settled into the bowl. You should count to 8-10 for the thick icing for the outline before it smoothes out with the rest of the icing. Thinner icing should take 5-8 seconds. If it is too thick just add a VERY little amount of water at a time and if it is too thin just add a little powdered sugar. (You can cheat and make a medium consistency (about 7 seconds) for the outline and the inside of the shape.)

Dye icing if you want a specific color (Americolor Soft Gel Paste).

Transfer icing to a piping bag or mini squeeze bottle. Wilton's sells ketchup bottle type containers that are nice and easy to use, or you can use piping bags. Use a Wilton #3 tip for the outline and a Wilton #5 for the filling. Royal Icing will harden quickly so ALWAYS keep your icing covered, including your piping bags. Place a wet paper towel at the bottom of a tall glass so the tip of the piping bag stays wet.

To get that 3D/layered effect, wait until the bottom coat is dry before adding details.

Do not refrigerate unused icing; just keep it in a tightly sealed container.

Pistachio Cake with Almond Glaze

My sister's favorite cake

Ingredients

Cake

- 1 box of yellow cake mix
- 1 box of instant pistachio pudding
- Eggs (see box instructions)
- Vegetable Oil (see box instructions)
- ½ teaspoon almond extract
- 7 drops green food coloring

Directions

Preheat oven to 350° F. Grease and flour a 10 inch tube pan.

In a large bowl, mix the dry ingredients.

Make a well in the center and pour in the rest of the ingredients (the "wet" ingredients). Blend all, and then beat for 2 minutes at medium speed.

Pour into prepared pan. Bake for 50 to 55 minutes, or until cake springs back when lightly pressed. Cool in pan 15 minutes. Flip over onto a wire rack and cool completely.

Ingredients

Almond Glaze

- 2 cups powdered sugar
- 2 tablespoons milk

1 tablespoon almond extract

Directions

Combine all ingredients and pour over the cake. Top with crushed pistachios.

Let Them Eat Cake!

My mother often baked and decorated wedding cakes for friends and family members when I was growing up. My sister and I would delight in watching her and waiting for the frosting flowers and bits of leveled cake to sample. We watched her measure and place toothpicks and slice off the uneven bits on top (to create a flat level ideal for frosting and decorating). It was the 1980s, so many cakes had vibrant colored frosting flowers and plastic staircases connecting one cake to another. Some even had working fountains underneath, with dyed water to match. I remember one wedding in which the dance floor was jumping, literally, and someone had the presence of mind to hold the tiered cake in place, to keep it from collapsing due to the crazy disco dancing.

Is it any wonder that I hold cake high above the other desserts? Even crème brûlée. Cookies and brownies are just a bit boring to me, compared to a layered, filled, frosted and decorated cake. I do like the cake-like cookies, such as a nice Black and White, or a Whoopie Pie (which is so not even a pie). Ice Box Cake is really a trifle, but it's made with graham crackers (which are more like cookies than crackers, am I right?) I do think that Oreo sandwich cookies are a modern derivative of Whoopie Pies, though unfortunately thinned, dried and shrunken for the convenience of modern industry and consumption. I do like the crushed Oreos in Dirt Cake (which is really a pudding), or in a nice Cookies and Cream ice cream.

I love to discover that ingredients can be substituted for another. Brown sugar can be made from sugar and cornstarch. Buttermilk can be made from vinegar and milk. Sweet coconut alcohol from your island can be substituted with palm vinegar or a delicate white wine. Sugar can be substituted with applesauce. Tapioca flour, which is gluten-free, can be substituted for white flour. Rice flour can be used for ground rice. Egg rolls can be used instead of pasta noodles.

Even more exciting is intermixing ethnic styles. I like to prepare enchiladas in the style of lasagna. Are they not both meat in a starch with tomato sauce and cheese? I like pasta carbonara like a stir-fry. The Brazilian cheese balls are strikingly similar to an Asian pastry, and by the way, these are both naturally gluten- free variations of the basic French pastry dough. And really, aren't Mexican Wedding Cookies and Russian Tea Cakes the same?

But, back to the cake. (And it is always about the cake.) I remember attending my friend's wedding and thinking, "Wow, those cakes are unusually tall." Turns out, the filling between each layer was an actual cheesecake. And that was a match made in heaven.

Black Forest Cake

Ingredients:

1 Devil's Food Cake Mix

*Ingredients per the cake mix, such as eggs, oil, and water

1 jar maraschino cherries

1 can cherry pie filling

2 canisters almond vanilla frosting (or white)

Chocolate sprinkles optional

Directions:

Prepare the chocolate cake in two round pans, as directed on the box.

After cakes are cooled, prep one onto the serving plate. You will need to flip it over so that the flat side is on the bottom.

Pipe a ¼-inch thick tube of frosting around the inside edge of the top of the cake. This is to secure the filling. If you don't have decorator tips, do not worry. Just use a plastic sandwich bag, and cut a small hole out of the bottom.

Pour and spread the cherry pie filling on top of the cake, within the frosting border. Place the next cake on top, so that the flat side is on the top. If needed, add frosting and/or filling at this time.

Frost the cake with the almond vanilla/ white frosting. Decorate with whole maraschino cherries and chocolate sprinkles.

Drunken Cakes

I have never been drunk, and I am okay with that. This is not to say that I don't enjoy a little wine here and there. I just don't see the appeal in getting so sick you can't think straight. (I have endured an epic gall bladder attack, after nine months of attacks, so I'm good. Did you want to know what color the vomit was? I didn't think so. Okay, then.) I recently discovered flavored Kombucha (fermented tea), which kind of reminds me of the Bacardi Breezers we drank in college.

I like a little Kahlua in my coffee, and I like a lot of alcohol in my cakes. Have you ever tasted a Harvey Wallbanger cake? Can you imagine? My mom makes this sometimes. Her Crème de Menthe cupcakes are legendary in our family. Remember the alcohol bakes out. But still. There is a strong alcoholic fragrance to this cake. If you happen to be eating some of these cupcakes after a high school powder puff game and see a sobriety checkpoint coming up on the Boulevard, you may want to take another route. I'm just sayin'.

On my mother's island of Guam, there is a special coconut alcohol made from the sap of the coconut tree, called tuba. Not like the musical instrument, you pronounce it by pulling your tongue away from the back of your top teeth, making a thick "TU" sound, followed by a short, staccato "bah!" TU-bah'. Farmers collect the sap and allow it to ferment. This becomes a sweet tuba liqueur. It's famous. The locals can handle it, but they love to tease the Haolies (non-islanders) with it. Haolies do not seem to be able to handle this naturally fermented drink. Of course, they all think they can, which provide endless entertainment for the islanders. It's the combination of having drunk tuba and beer (separately) that churns the stomach so that you will be sick and worthless for up to three days. My Haolie dad should know better! He's been married to an island girl for nearly fifty years! But it happened to him not too long ago.

I am not trying this. It takes two days to get to Guam (14 hours of flight passing over the International Date Line) and another day to get back home to California. I am not spending half of my week-long vacation sick in bed.

But I love potu (POH-tu'), which is a sweet sticky rice cake made with tuba. Here on the mainland we make it with alternate wines.

But if you find yourself on Guam, I dare you to try the tuba. While riding a caribou.

Only on Guam.

Potu

(Sweet Rice Cake from Guam)

The original recipes call for pre-soaking the rice in tuba, the alcoholic fermented coconut sap from the island of Guam. You can use Palm Vinegar and Rice Flour for the quick and easy way.

I use my favorite sweet wine: Gewürztraminer.

Ingredients

    1 cup rice flour (must be non-glutinous)

    ¾ cup sugar

    1½ tablespoons baking powder

    4 tablespoons vinegar mixed with water to equal 1 cup of liquid (OR use 1 cup sweet tuba) Or Gewürztraminer

Instructions

    Mix all ingredients in a bowl and let it sit for about 15 minutes.

    Pour the mixture into foil cupcake liners or silicone molds and steam for about 15-20 minutes.

Crème de Menthe Cake

Ingredients

- 1 box yellow cake mix
- 1 package instant lemon pudding
- 1 package whipped topping
- ¼ cup cooking oil
- 4 eggs
- 1 cup Crème de Menthe

Directions

Mix all ingredients together and beat 2 minutes.

Pour batter into well-greased and lightly floured Bundt pan.

Bake at 350° for 45-50 minutes.

Dash with powdered sugar or frost with your favorite glaze.

Savory

Marina Restaurant

The sweet, light blue house sits at the edge of the water, near all the sailboats parked on the westward pier. Sunset affords a special view, with the airplanes of the bay area's three airports landing and taking off. The planes appear to be gliding in blue water like fish. At night, the holiday lights strung among them sparkle like auxiliary stars. There's a particularly special table for two near the window, with tall, upholstered armchairs where you feel like royalty. And until recently, there used to be a single table on the "second floor." A table for ten lofting atop the private staircase and affording views of the bustling restaurant below, as well as of the magnificent sunset, marina lights, boats and flying fishes. The décor is dark wood nautical, making you feel as if you are sailing the seven seas. It's a long way off the freeway and down Marina Boulevard, but so worth it. And the food is simply divine.

So many special occasions were celebrated here: birthdays, anniversaries, Mother's Day. I remember my mother saying it was her favorite restaurant when I was growing up. I brought my husband once, and now we celebrate many of our occasions there. When you call to make your reservation, they ask if you are celebrating an event, and if so, they offer you a complimentary crème brûlée, plated with a chocolate greeting. (Except once when I said I would be celebrating my promotion. They didn't offer a complimentary dessert then. I suppose they figured I could afford my fancy dessert!)

Join me now, as we dine. The bread is a buttery, garlicky, earthen flatbread. You must begin with the Maytag Blue Cheese salad, a family favorite, decorated with almond slivers. (Though be aware, in recession years, there is noticeably less blue cheese.) Our favorite appetizers include the teriyaki filet mignon tenderloin coins, and the outstanding roasted crab and artichoke dip (which is normally served on sandwiches for lunch), and the warm Brie with macadamia nut crust. You should be so lucky as to taste the salmon bisque, it's not offered every night, and sometimes they run out of salmon if they are serving the bisque. You are in a seafood restaurant overlooking the bay, please enjoy asiago-almond crusted scallops or petite lobster tail alongside creamy and chunky mashed potatoes, or maybe crab and macadamia nut stuffed halibut. But my personal favorite is the filet mignon, and I cannot go and not order it. I like it medium rare, with asparagus on the side. Delicious with my favorite Red Diamond Merlot.

And now, for our dessert. Somebody in your party must be celebrating a special occasion, without exception. Then you begin the dessert course with their famous crème brûlée, or maybe a slice of Key Lime pie if you prefer. Then order a slice of heaven in the chocolate indulgence cake, or go crazy with the Bananas Foster Sundae—enjoying the caramelized banana, buttermilk waffle, vanilla ice cream, candied pecans, and house made butterscotch sauce poured tableside. My personal favorite was the Baked Alaska, which included a layer of mango puree beneath the meringue and over the vanilla ice cream.

What did you think? Want to join me there for your next special occasion? Elsewhere in this book, I'll detail my dream dinner, which is inspired in part by the restaurant on the Marina. But for now, you can try my copycat recipe for the Maytag Blue Cheese Salad. *Bon Appetit!*

Blue Cheese Salad

Ingredients:

    Romaine lettuce

    2 eggs, hard-boiled

    Almond slivers

    Blue cheese dressing

    Blue cheese crumbles

Directions:

At the restaurant they served it cold, but we like to have freshly hard-boiled eggs, because the warmth kind of melts the cheese just a little. I add a lot of all the items. If you don't like thick dressing, you can thin it with red wine vinegar.

    Toss the lettuce

    Slice the hard-boiled eggs into slivers.

    Add the eggs and cheese crumbles to the salad.

    Toss the salad again.

    Add dressing

    Garnish with almonds.

Sweet Pairings

Sometimes the boys stay home to watch football so my daughter and I go out and do all the girl things. These things include but are not limited to -- manicures, pedicures, haircuts, clothes shopping, art supplies shopping, coffee shop visit, and a fancy brunch. Wouldn't you rather come with me? I thought so. We are quite the pair.

One of our favorite little restaurants is about half an hour away, in a cutesy uppity downtown shopping district with a clock tower and old-timey candy store. The first time we went to this place, she was so young and delighted to be in a fancy restaurant on a brunch date with just Mommy. The reason we chose this restaurant, The Peasant and the Pear, was due to its delightful name, and specialty of pears. How sweet is that?

We began with their famous fondue: New York white cheddar. It came bubbling and purring in a sweet little black iron cauldron served with bread, grapes, and pears. My daughter wouldn't stop smiling as she dove into the pears and grapes then dunked them in the thick potion. (I usually serve fondue with vegetables and meats at home, though she doesn't particularly care for the cherry tomato, simply stating that they are "Too squirty.")

The fondue is so indulgent, it almost seems silly proceeding to the entrée. She typically enjoys either a grilled cheese sandwich or maybe macaroni and cheese from the Little Gourmand menu, because one can never have too much cheese. Right? (At least she didn't order alphabet soup, like that one time on the cruise ship with a $25 cover charge for the specialty restaurant!) I like to get the black and bleu salad, which consists of pan-seared filet mignon tips, Point Reyes bleu cheese on Romaine lettuce with blue cheese dressing and crispy fried onions atop. The steak is warm, and the lettuce is cool. The onion topping is just the right amount of crunch.

And because we cannot skip dessert, we love sharing crème brûlée. There is something so satisfying about making that first crack in the glassy caramelized sugar atop the creamy vanilla bean custard. My daughter usually giggles at this part, and I can't help but giggle, too. She is, after all, my inner child. The apple (or pear, in this case) doesn't fall too far from the tree.

Fondue

Many years ago, I remember seeing a recipe for fondue on a Campbell's Cheddar Cheese Soup can. I couldn't seem to find it online. So here is what I make from memory. Sounds weird, I know, but it's actually pretty good. My family really enjoys it, although husband thinks it's high in calories, so he only likes me to cook it once a year. But this is the BEST way to get children to eat vegetables. I'm certain there are classier recipes out there, but this one suits a young family just fine!

Ingredients:

1 can Campbell's Cheddar Cheese Soup

1 soup can-full of milk (about 8 oz.)

½ cup to 1 cup apple juice or white wine (as you prefer)

8 oz. sour cream

1 cup to 2 cups Swiss cheese (as you prefer)

Directions:

Combine ingredients over stovetop in a large deep pot, such as your pasta pot.

Cut sourdough bread into one inch cubes.

Serve with homemade Italian meatballs and steamed broccoli. I like those cocktail "smokies"" for this, too. Cauliflower, whatever else you can think of.

NOTE: I like to scoop big spoonfuls of the fondue into individual ramekins. Then it is like we each have our own little fondue pot. Then, when there's leftover sauce, I pour it over cooked pasta to make macaroni and cheese. Delish!

To Spam or Not to Spam

My mom was born on the island of Guam during World War II as the youngest of seven children. Growing up post-war on the east side of the Pacific Ocean, one of the staples of Guam meals became spam. Yes, SPAM, the pink "meat". Meanwhile, my dear father was living in San Francisco, the oldest son of six children and his mother found an inexpensive way to feed the family in the years post-war was spam. Is it any wonder then that these two found each other?

I don't love spam. (I love salami, but that's different.) I remember eating spam as a child. It was fried and served with titiyas (see page 131 for this fabulous flatbread recipe). I have never eaten, prepared, nor served spam ever in my adult life. Because of this story.

It was 1976 and I was so excited to be getting my first pet, a cat. I was five years old. My father had spoken to the cat lady who said she was holding the black cat with special white markings for me. We just needed to eat our dinner first and then we could go.

But my mom had made spam that night. It was diced, fried spam with frozen peas in tomato sauce over rice. Seriously. I know most of you are reading this right now, thinking to yourself, YUCK! When I mentioned to my sweet parents that I would be writing about this dish, my father burst out with "Delicious!" I am so serious right now. Anyway. Even as a kid in the 70's I knew this was weird. My younger sister didn't like peas, and I didn't like spam, so it was a bad deal. We threatened not to eat and they threatened not to get the cat. My sister cannot deal with peas, even to this very day. Our parents actually left the kitchen after they had finished eating, and we girls sat there counting minutes and holding forks with food dangling, but not eating. Spam is so weird; it's a pink, salty, greasy, questionable protein. The meal seemed to take forever -- and I know it did, because when we finally went to the cat lady's house to pick up my new kitten, it was very, very, very dark outside.

So, you will NOT find a spam recipe in this collection.

You're welcome.

Seconds Pasta

This is a go-to meal for my family. It used to be called "Chicken Apple Sausage Pasta with Pesto and Pine Nuts" but that was too long to say. I just call it Seconds Pasta now, because it is so quick to make, and everyone always wants seconds. You'll see why, I promise.

Now everyone knows what I am talking about when I say Seconds Pasta. I've made it so often that I've perfected it to a one-pot prep in 15 minutes. (It really helps when you purchase the ingredients in bulk at your big box store.) One time when I ran out of grated cheese, I improvised by dicing mozzarella sticks. The kids loved it, and called them "cheese bombs." And now they won't have it any other way.

Ingredients:

1 package pasta

5 mozzarella cheese sticks

5 Aidell's Chicken Apple sausages

¼ cup pine nuts

⅓ jar of Pesto Sauce (about 7 ounces)

Directions:

Toast pine nuts in pasta bowl over high heat. When they start to get a little brown, move them to a small bowl. In same pasta bowl, boil water. While the water boils and pasta cooks, dice the sausages and cheese sticks.

Drain pasta when ready. Move pasta to serving bowl. Cook the sausage pieces. The pot is already hot, so it cooks fast.

Toss the pasta back in, along with the cheese pieces. The

cheese will start melting.

Toss in the pine nuts and pesto. Stir so that all the pasta is coated in pesto. Serve in serving bowl.

The Magic of Cheese

My friends, let me just tell you straight up that it is really, really hard to write about cheese, without, you know, getting cheesy. Here goes nothing.

I love cheese. Almost about as much as I love bread. But cheesy bread is the best. Alas, I digress. I remember when my parents got our first microwave oven when my sister and I were kids. We would put grated mozzarella on a microwave-safe plate and cook it for about thirty seconds; we then ate the melted cheese with a fork. All right, I still do that sometimes, late at night when I'm too lazy to even make a quesadilla. OK, I had it last night. Hey. Don't knock it until you've tried it! (Italian six cheese blend is the best.) #glutenfreequesadilla

Once I made homemade mac and cheese for a pool party. I told a horrified skinny mom there that I had put 4 cups of shredded cheese in it. It was awkward. She then asked me with a feeble voice, "Well, at least you used the turkey smokies instead of the beef ones...?" Seriously. What? I felt sorry for her. Because she obviously didn't know the magic of cheese.

My daughter would have macaroni and cheese every day, if I let her. If she doesn't want to eat roast beef, we just put cheese on it for her. I remember our first day in Rome last summer, and she ordered a grilled cheese sandwich at a café across from the Colosseum. It was mozzarella on ciabatta, and the melted cheese just stretched and stretched after she took a bite: about twelve inches across the table, just like the noodle scene in *Lady and the Tramp*. We were all delighted right along with her!

Adding just a bit of cheese to scrambled eggs is a wonderful trick. Ricotta or cream cheese will make you exclaim: IT'S SO FLUFFY!

There was only one time that I hesitated to have cheese. Two by four inch bricks of cheddar cheese floating in a dense orange cheese sauce, known as Broiled Cheese Bricks were offered in my college dorm cafeteria. Yeah, I thought that was a bit much.

But other than that, I'll always say, Pass the cheese, please!

Mac 'N Cheese

Inspired by a recipe in the *Mommy Made and Daddy Too* cookbook.

I once brought this simple crowd favorite to a potluck. No one had thought to bring forks, so people used tortilla chips to scoop it up.

Ingredients:

½ pound macaroni, cooked according to package directions

4 cups grated sharp cheddar cheese

1 cup milk

3 tablespoon parmesan cheese

Directions:

Preheat oven to 350°.

Cook and drain macaroni and toss with cheddar cheese.

Heat milk over medium until hot, then add to macaroni and cheese. Season with salt and pepper if desired. Mix to blend. Pour into eight-inch square glass or ceramic baking dish. Sprinkle with parmesan cheese.

Bake for 15 minutes or until bubbly. Allow to sit for 5 to 10 minutes before serving.

Optional Toppings:

Breadcrumbs

1 lb. ground meat, cooked and seasoned.

1 package cocktail "smokies" (mini smoked sausages)

Zucchini slices

Tofu

Hot dog slices

Hyperlexic Parenting

My life journey includes the blessing and honor of raising a child on the Autism Spectrum. I'm not gonna lie, when your child is first diagnosed, it is like the rug is pulled from under you. But honestly, we are so lucky to enjoy adventures and creative thinking. Teaching and learning, learning and teaching. We figure it out together. Through speech therapy, we realized that our two-year-old son had the ability to read. Hello, Hyperlexia. Letters and numbers became our friends. He said "Wes," for Yes. Why? Because the word "Why" starts with the letter W. Get it?

So my quirky kid didn't like veggies when he was younger, until Auntie Rachel told him that corn had Vitamin A in it. (Why didn't I think of that? Tell a hyperlexic child that he can EAT a letter by having veggies... brilliant.) He then quickly decided that he was a CORN MONSTER! (Like Cookie Monster.) Soon, even "skinny baby carrots" (raw) were okay.

I used to have to blend boiled carrots into his applesauce (the Magic Bullet is a wonderful invention.) Or, we'd resort to carrot juice and tomato juice. (Sometimes, though, he still fake-gags in protest of the carrots.)

One night he sat with "skinny baby carrots" before him and I had a big bowl of my mom's recipe for cucumber salad. The kid stared intently at me and I asked him, "Do you want some?" He answered, "Wes."

He loved it. Then he pushed away the skinny baby carrots and reached for more cucumbers. And more and more. Who would have thought this beautiful quirky and finicky kid would love something doused in vinegar and soy sauce?

Cucumber and Soy Sauce Salad

(Great with Asian meals)

Ingredients:

1 thinly sliced English cucumber,

1 teaspoon garlic salt,

1 tablespoon Soy Sauce, and

White Vinegar or Rice Vinegar to taste.

Directions:

Toss all ingredients in a bowl and serve.

For the Love of Salami

I know I said I can't deal with spam, but I love salami. It's different. It is. Okay, it is also a pinkish curated meat, salty, and greasy, but to me it has always been a veritable protein. My kids love salami, too, much to my husband's dismay. And he's Italian! I know! The first time I cooked for him, when we had only just started dating, I decided to make a pasta salad since I knew he was Italian. He took out the tomatoes, mushrooms, olives, artichoke hearts, and salami. So basically, he ate pasta and vinaigrette. Oh, and cheese. (You can never have too much cheese.)

Anyway, back to the salami. Sometimes when I just feel like "snack-y dinner" we have salami, and cheese and crackers. If I need to bring a protein or snack to a team event, I slice mozzarella sticks in half and wrap with a slice of salami, and secure with a toothpick. My young daughter thinks this is "fancy." I prefer salami on a pizza to pepperoni. Sometimes I use it instead of bacon in "Ferghetti and Hammer" (see page 106).

When I was nine years old, my family travelled to Guam and Japan in 1980. We took a five-week family vacation: two weeks in Japan, two weeks in Guam, and one more week in Japan. My young sister and I were finicky eaters at best, and our doting mom was worried about what food might be available for us that we would actually eat, so she brought along a log of hard salami, wrapped in the whitish casing. We must have eaten a lot of salami those first two weeks, being wholly unaccustomed to Japanese food. I remember eating salami on the airplane. It was our salvation. The first meal we had together in Japan was a total waste of our money. There was horseradish spread over every surface. We would just sit there and try not to look at it. Egg salad sandwiches with peas, and horseradish. You would think that pepperoni pizza at a familiar American pizza chain might be safe, but it was doused with anchovies and sardines, etc.

When my own family was in Barcelona last summer, we were delighted to find a tapas place right along the beach in Barceloneta, the gorgeous sunny and sandy beach area of the city of Barcelona. We tried a few different things, but once my family saw there was a salami baguette on the menu, four of the seven of us ordered it. Coincidentally, it was one of our favorite times of our Mediterranean cruise. But maybe that could have been the Sangria, as well.

Caprese Denisi

(Great with Italian meals)

Ingredients:

Sliced Roma tomatoes

Sliced Mozzarella cheese

Julienne sliced salami (this is the Denisi part)

1 tablespoon Extra Virgin Olive Oil

1 tablespoon Balsamic or red wine vinegar

Basil for garnish (fresh or dry)

Directions:

Lay alternate tomatoes, mozzarella, and julienned salami slices onto a plate.

Drizzle olive oil then sprinkle balsamic or red wine vinegar to taste.

Cousins

Nobody believes me when I say that I have forty-two first cousins. It's true. My mother is the baby of seven children, and my father is one of six. So, my sister and I have forty-two first cousins. And that's not even all of them. My dad has always been very close to his own first cousins, and therefore we are close to their kids (our second cousins -- twelve of them). And on Guam, everybody is a "cousin" -- someone who is related to someone who is related to you.

Our husbands come from small families, and they have maybe five cousins apiece. This is more typical for American families. My own children have a total of four cousins, but I am so happy that they are so close to all of their cousins. There is a special bond among cousins, especially of a similar age. We are like both friends and siblings. We are family.

I have been so lucky to enjoy a particular friendship with several of my cousins. Nowadays, the cousins, aunts and uncles participate in a "pick-em" fantasy football league, called the Westwood Challenge, named after the street where my grandfather and great-aunt once lived. It is exciting that my son and other 3rd generation kids participate, too. I also love when one of the cousins gets married. It's like getting a new cousin!

Brie en Cruste

Recipe from my cousins Dan & Stacy

Ingredients:

1 wheel Brie cheese (cut off the white rinds)

1 cylindrical package crescent roll dough

1 tablespoon raspberry jam (more to taste!)

Directions:

Preheat oven to 350°.

Place Brie in rolled out crescent roll dough.

Scoop raspberry jam on top of Brie.

Fold edges of dough on top.

Bake for 20 minutes.

Serve hot with bread or crackers of choice. (I like wheat crackers best).

One of These Things is Not Like the Other

I was baptized at the Church of the Holy Spirit. My first real music director position was at another Holy Spirit Church. Of the three parts of the Holy Trinity, I have always been most drawn to the Holy Spirit. For me, the Holy Spirit allows for so many wonderful things to come together, to make sense.

There was this one time I was in music ministry for a Mass of the Holy Spirit. In academic environments, this is a special way to commence the school year. At Santa Clara University, this mass was held outdoors, in the Rose Garden. There is a covered walkway people can stroll through that is part of the original structure that acts as a lovely natural barrier between the two parts of the garden.

On this particular sunny afternoon, the Mass of the Holy Spirit was on one side, and there was a wedding reception on the other. This was poor, planning on the part of the university because while we were celebrating mass, praying and singing, the other party was dancing to disco music provided by the DJ. I remember the moment the music started. I suspected the DJ thought we were, I don't know, praying too loudly, or something, so he turned the music up. I can totally see how a DJ would be like, "Oh are they reading the Bible out loud over there? We don't wanna hear that! Let's crank up this baby!" Honest, it was all I could do to focus on our mass because part of me wanted to be over there dancing.

Then it was my turn to start playing electric piano, for the entire congregation to sing the Psalm. This particular Psalm was one of my favorites—a kind of Baptist-styled, spirited number—very appropriate for the Holy Spirit, but not for the disco-dancing wedding party from over the wall. "Knock on Wood." By Amii Stewart. Boom. Boom. Boom.

I summoned all the discipline I could muster, and began playing the intro to our Psalm, pretending that disco music wasn't pounding nearby. "Holy Spirit, I prayed, silently and frantically, If there was ever a time, please be with me now! Help me focus and play this song without messing up royally."

I focused on the black and white sheet music in front of me, and let my fingers fly. The choir sang and the people joined in on the refrain: "To You, O God, I Lift Up My Soul." I honestly don't know how I pulled it off…but for the power of the Holy Spirit.

This is why I do music ministry. The very nature of worship music is like an inspiring prayer. Even when I am nervous, I can just remember to focus on the words that I am singing, and it becomes my prayer. St. Augustine said, "To sing is to pray twice." As the famous Christian hymn says: *How can I keep from singing?*

And I highly doubt that the University will ever schedule an outdoor Mass adjoining a wedding reception again.

Cannelloni

(Updated from my mother-in-law's recipe)

Ingredients:

1 package Won Ton Wraps! (Square egg rolls - about 16 squares)

1 10 oz. package frozen chopped spinach

2 ½ teaspoon salt

¼ cup water

6 tablespoons butter

1 ½ lbs. ground beef

1 teaspoon crushed coriander

¼ teaspoon pepper

5 tablespoons flour

1 package (or one cube) beef broth

1 ¼ cups fat free half and half

2 cups grated Mozzarella cheese (or Italian cheese blend)

Directions:

Preheat oven to 350°. Thaw spinach in microwave. Drain well. Chop or use food processor to chop finely.

In large skillet, add 3 teaspoons butter. Stir in ground beef. Sprinkle with salt. Cook slowly until meat loses pink color but is not browned.

Add spinach and stir. Stir in coriander, pepper, and 2 tablespoons flour. Stirring constantly, one minute or until thick.

Spoon ⅓ cup meat filling in each square. Place a single layer in baking dish (9x13).

Returning to same skillet, melt remaining butter. Stir in remaining flour and beef broth (envelope or cube mixed with ½ cup boiling water.)

Cook, stirring constantly, one minute until bubbly. Stir in half and half. Continue stirring until sauce thickens. Boil one minute. (If too thin, add flour, butter. If too thick, add water.)

Pour over filled cannelloni. Cover with grated Mozzarella. Bake for 20 minutes until cheese melts.

BONUS RECIPE:

What do you do with the leftover egg rolls? Make chips!

Cut egg rolls into six square "chips." Lay on foil covered cookie sheet.

Sprinkle grated cheese on each chip.

Bake at 350° for two to five minutes until cheese bubbles, melts, and chips start to brown.

Meatloaf

My dad's favorite meal is meatloaf. I remember my grandma serving it with mashed potatoes and her creamed spinach. I like creamed spinach now, but I sure as all heck didn't want any of that stuff when I was a kid. I remember once serving myself the teeniest possible amount onto my plate, just to be polite. My grandfather said to me, "Did you use an eyedropper, Denise?"

My grandma's creamed spinach was frozen chopped spinach cooked with "White Sauce" from a jar. My mother replicates it by making her own white sauce, which includes hard-boiled eggs? I don't even know. I remember detecting the egg whites and thinking, "That's weird."

We live in California, where everybody knows we are experiencing a meta-season called Drought. Whenever it rains, or even if the forecast shows a small chance of rain, I am planning to bake meatloaf. I suppose it stems from not wanting to use the oven during the already hot weather.

I have developed a kind of meatball-loaf for my family. It is a basic meatball recipe, but in the shape of a loaf. I put the tomato paste and cheese inside the meatball loaf, for extra flavor through and through.

My family is always so excited when I announce that I going to make meatloaf for dinner. But I won't ever order meatloaf when we go out. It's just not the same. You'll see.

Meatball Loaf

Ingredients:

1½ pounds ground beef

1 large egg

1 grated onion (optional)

½ cup chopped flat-leaf parsley (or prepared Italian spices)

½ cup bread crumbs (make your own)

½ cup grated Parmesan or Italian cheese combination

¼ cup tomato paste (or pizza sauce)

salt

pepper

Milk (optional)

Directions:

Preheat oven to 400°.

Place the ground beef in a large bowl, arrange so that there is a well the middle. This is where you will dump all the other ingredients. In another bowl, break a slice of bread into crumbs. Add egg, onion, parsley or Italian seasoning, and cheese to the big bowl. Add the breadcrumbs, and if you like, about one tablespoon of milk. Now add the tomato paste, and season with salt and pepper. Mix all of this together using your hands. It will be quite messy! Of course, you can add more of everything, to your taste. Just make sure to add more egg, tomato paste, or milk if you are adding a lot of dry ingredients. You want the loaf to retain its shape and not become too dry and crumbly.

On a foil-lined baking sheet, form the mixture into an loaf, it should be about 3 inches high and four inches wide, maybe about 8 inches long. Bake until cooked through, 40 to 50 minutes.

Italian Meatballs

Ingredients

Same ingredients as meatloaf:

1½ pounds ground beef

1 large egg

1 grated onion (optional)

½ cup chopped flat-leaf parsley (or prepared Italian spices)

½ cup bread crumbs (make your own)

½ cup grated Parmesan or Italian cheese combination

¼ cup tomato paste (or pizza sauce)

salt

pepper

Milk (optional)

Directions

Preheat oven at 350°

Combine all ingredients and roll into 2-inch balls.

Place in casserole dish. Place in oven and bake for 15 minutes.

Doesn't it seem that everything is always 350° for fifteen minutes?

Dump the pre-made sauce of your choice in to the saucepan. I like a Cabernet marinara. Place the cooked meatballs into the sauce. Simmer for like five to ten minutes. Separately, prepare cheese tortellini.

Uncle Pat's Meatballs

(a more traditional recipe)

Ingredients

1 ½ lbs. ground beef or turkey

1 large egg

1 cup flavored breadcrumbs

Optional: peppers, onions, garlic and basil, mixed in food processor

1 jar spaghetti sauce

Directions

Mix ingredients together and form into meatballs.

Fry in olive oil to brown. It is not necessary to cook all the way through.

Season spaghetti sauce with garlic and oregano (or Italian seasoning)

Add meatballs to the sauce. Simmer for one hour.

Scandalous! Unpopular Opinion

You know that I am a grateful gal. There are so many blessings in my life.

My husband loves Thanksgiving. It's his favorite holiday: food, family, football, four-day weekend, and he doesn't have to go to church or exchange gifts.

I confess: Thanksgiving is NOT my favorite holiday, because of the food.

[Insert needle jumping off vinyl record here.]

WHAT?

I realize this is an unpopular opinion, which is why I have kept it secret for 34 years. Alas, I simply cannot stand it any longer. THE TRUTH MUST BE SET FREE!

I like turkey. I like *real* cranberry sauce. I just think the traditional trimmings with all the fatty starchy carbohydrates, not to mention all the bland mushy similarly boring taste(s) and texture(s), are plain as baby food to me.

One year I was blessed to share Thanksgiving dinner four times within five days. Like I said, I am a grateful gal. Among countless blessings, I am very lucky to have opportunities to visit and dine with three superior hostesses (and not have to cook, myself.). You know, it was one set of parents, and the other, and then said parents' favorite neighbors, and then the obligatory leftovers. Oh. My. God. Make it stop! (Don't even get me started on the vat of cornflake cheese potato casserole that someone brought one year.) Break a successful stream of healthy eating habits for this? I just don't think it's worth it. I'd much prefer a filet mignon, medium rare in a merlot sauce, baked asparagus with Parmesan cheese, and bruschetta on toasted sourdough followed by a respectable amount of chocolate. And I'd be just as thankful, if not more.

Roman Beans

Adapted from the *Good Housekeeping Cookbook*. I made this once for Thanksgiving at the in-laws' and now they ask for it every year. As we say in liturgical music school, if the people like it, it's a "tradition," right?

Ingredients:

    2 lb. fresh green beans

    4 oz. bacon cut crosswise into ½-inch strips

    1 tablespoon olive oil

    ½ teaspoon salt

    ¼ cup pine nuts

Directions:

Toss the pine nuts in the skillet without any additional oil. Using a wooden spoon, toss until they are slightly toasted. Set aside.

In 12-inch skillet (at least 2 inches deep) or 5-quart saucepot over high heat, in one-inch boiling water, heat green beans to boiling.

Reduce heat to low; simmer 5-10 minutes until beans are tender-crisp; drain. Wipe skillet dry.

In same skillet over medium heat, cook bacon until golden, stirring frequently. With slotted spoon, remove bacon to paper towels to drain. OR, do this: cook the bacon in the microwave over paper towels. Allow one minute for each strip. The bacon is extra crispy this way, and not fatty. I think it adds a nice texture to the dish.

In same skillet over medium-high heat, in drippings and olive oil, cook green beans with salt, stirring frequently, until beans are lightly browned and tender.

Spoon green beans onto warm large platter; sprinkle with bacon and toasted pine nuts.

Filet Mignon & Red Wine Sauce

Ingredients

2 filet mignon steaks: about 8 ounces each

Your favorite seasonings, such as garlic salt and black pepper

Butter

Merlot, or Your Favorite Red Wine

Directions

Preheat oven to 425°

Season all sides of the thick cuts. Melt 1 tablespoon. butter in frying pan. Sear both sides of the steaks 2-3 minutes each side. Transfer steaks to oven. Bake for about 15 minutes for medium-rare (145° internal temperature). Use a meat thermometer.

Using same searing pan, remove from heat. Add ½ cup Merlot (or your favorite red wine). Return to heat. Boil until reduced to half volume. Add two tablespoons butter, stir until butter melts.

Plate the filet mignon and drizzle the merlot sauce atop.

Serve alongside green vegetables.

Follow with decadent dessert.

The Trouble with Chicken

I don't love chicken. My mom endured the Scarsdale diet that was all the rage in the 1980s, and she'd gotten tired of it. Meanwhile, my father who is really a meat and potatoes guy (who loves spam) didn't complain. And outside of some KFC here and there, I found that I could live a happy life without chicken. Then in high school, I would often enjoy dinner at my boyfriend's house with his family, and they had chicken all the time. I seriously thought, "Wow, they must be rich!"

Some of my husband's favorite meals are chicken entrees. Unfortunately my daughter is like me, and doesn't love chicken, either. So I don't make his favorites meals often. My daughter loves popcorn chicken, "but not the white part."

Uh, the CHICKEN?

Right.

My son likes chicken, though. So I do every once in a while, prepare one of my dear husband's favorites. To a mixed audience. My husband loves it, my son likes it, and my daughter cries in protest when we make her eat it. By the end of the meal, I'm so frazzled I haven't enjoyed eating the meal, myself.

I once made the savory chicken squares (page __). My kids were close by watching my preparation and I figured I should get them involved. I thought I was totally selling my daughter on this meal because of the cream cheese in the filling and the croissant dough we rolled out. She even liked her first bite! Success! Then I realized that bite had no chicken in it. Well, there's always next time.

In the meantime, I serve my daughter chicken apple sausage

and somehow that's okay because it looks like a hot dog. I don't even know. *Måsa i mannok!* (This chicken is done!)

Lemon Chicken Pesto

Ingredients:

2-4 pieces thawed boneless skinless chicken breasts

Juice of one lemon (bottled lemon juice is okay)

1 tub of pre-made pesto (about 7 ounces)

1 teaspoon Olive oil

Garlic to taste

Directions:

Dice the chicken prior to cooking so there is more surface for the pesto to grab onto.

Fry the diced chicken pieces with olive oil and lemon juice. Add garlic, to taste. When ready, scoop into big bowl.

Dump the pesto sauce (cold) into the bowl, and stir until the all the chicken is coated. The warmth of the freshly cooked chicken will warm up the pesto sauce.

Serving suggestions:

Parmesan Couscous (Near East brand packaged in a box) and a green veggie, like sautéed zucchini with parmesan or green beans with almonds. (This is dear husband's favorite meal.)

Savory Chicken Squares

Ingredients

- 1 package (3 oz.) cream cheese, softened
- 1 tablespoon butter, softened
- 2 cups cubed cooked chicken
- 1 tablespoon chopped fresh chives or onion (optional)
- ¼ teaspoon salt
- 1/8 teaspoon pepper
- 2 tablespoons milk
- 1 tablespoon sun-dried tomatoes
- 1 can (8 oz.) refrigerated crescent dinner rolls
- 1 tablespoon butter, melted
- ¾ cup seasoned croutons, crushed

Directions:

Heat oven to 350°F.

In medium bowl, mix cream cheese and 1 tablespoon softened butter; beat until smooth. Add everything else and mix well.

Separate or cut dough into 4 rectangles. You will need to overlap the perforated pieces, and use a rolling pin to smooth it out to make it thinner and bigger.

Spoon ½ cup chicken mixture onto center of each rectangle*.

Pull 4 corners of dough to center of chicken mixture; twist firmly. Pinch edges to seal.

Place on ungreased cookie sheet. Brush tops of sandwiches with 1 tablespoon melted butter; sprinkle with crushed croutons.

Bake 25 to 30 minutes or until golden brown.

*Sometimes I put scrambled eggs, cheese and ham into these croissant squares and call it brunch.

Easy Chicken Parmesan

Ingredients:

Chicken breasts

Equal parts grated Parmesan cheese and mayonnaise

Dash of Garlic Salt

French/Sourdough bread (optional)

Directions

Preheat oven to 350°

Mix ingredients to form a spread. Spread on top of chicken breast pieces.

Bake for about 20 to 25 minutes

Garlic Bread

If you have any extra of the parmesan/mayonnaise/ garlic salt mixture, spread it on bread and bake for 15 to 20 minutes.

Teriyaki Sticks

Come with me now to your favorite tropical island. Imagine the warm sun beaming down over the crystalline beach and sugary sand, as you gaze from your hammock strung between two palm trees. Take a sip now, from your favorite tropical drink in its cobalt blue glass and savor the flavor. Hear the soulful singing, ukulele, slack guitar and steel drums. A young islander brings you a gift of a platter of food, including barbeque meats thinly sliced and skewered on bamboo sticks. Are you with me? We are going to enjoy teriyaki sticks now!

Everybody talks about my sweet mother's wonderful teriyaki dinner. Her homemade teriyaki sauce is a delight to behold. The marinated steak kabobs are sweet and salty. As one of my dear friends exclaimed in amazement, "It's like candy!" There are legendary family stories on how many bamboo sticks my cousin left on his plate when he was a teenager: 42. Seriously. I know, it's the meaning of life.

The secret is in the presentation. Mom serves her teriyaki sticks with buttery white rice mixed with soy sauce, as well as pineapple slices and banana kabobs. The banana is sliced in the peel, and skewered along with the pineapple slices. The pineapple glistens and turns golden brown. You have to remove the banana from the skewer, and then sort of squeeze the peel to make the inside of the banana squish out into your mouth. It doesn't sound very sophisticated, but trust me when I say it is delightfully enjoyable. It tastes like a warm banana custard, or crème brûlée.

Teriyaki Marinade

Ingredients:

    ⅓ cup water

    ⅓ cup brown sugar

    ⅓ cup soy sauce

    1 teaspoon crushed garlic

    1 teaspoon ground ginger

Directions:

    In a medium bowl, mix water, brown sugar, soy sauce, garlic, and ginger.

    Place desired meat in the mixture.

    Cover, and marinate in the refrigerator at least two hours before grilling as desired.

Directions

For the teriyaki steak kabobs

    Slice ribeye steak in ¼ inch strips.

    Marinade the thin slices overnight.

    Skewer on sticks.

    Broil or grill for eight to ten minutes on each side.

    Serve with broiled banana and pineapple skewers, and buttery soy sauced white rice.

Bacon

I usually have to work on Christmas Eve, but my husband has the day off, so he spends the day with our kids. One year, my brother-in-law also had the day off and was with my nieces, so they met up for lunch. It is our custom that I go straight to church from work, as I am the designated seat-saver.

(Christmas Eve Family Mass is crazy crowded at my parish. For the ten of us, we need almost an entire pew.)

After Mass, we enjoy dinner together.

At dinner this one particular year, I asked my daughter if she had protein with her lunch. The four children said in unison: "Bacon." I asked her what her brother had. The children all responded again, "Bacon." I asked a third question, I don't even remember what it was, but it was a yes-or-no question, and the children answered with "Bacon."

Clearly, the new affirmative is, Bacon.

I kinda like it. Why say "Yes," when you can just say "Bacon!"?

One time the children's choir at church was performing a bright, spirited number entitled "Praise Him." My then four-year-old niece thought they were singing "BA-CON!" Because, of course. She perked up like it was the best song ever. "I like bacon! Do you like bacon? Why are they singing about bacon?"

The next recipe in this collection is Fergetti and Hammer. The peculiar name for this recipe is because when I was a young child, I couldn't say Spaghetti and Ham. It's based on the Italian spaghetti carbonara, but since my mom is from a

Pacific island, this version tastes more like a kind of stir-fry. And my kids and I would not have it any other way. The star of the following recipe is- (sing it with me now) BA-CON!

Ferghetti and Hammer

a.k.a Spaghetti Carbonara Stir-Fry

Ingredients:

1 pound dry spaghetti

2 tablespoons extra-virgin olive oil or butter

4 bacon slices, cooked until crisp. Chop and set aside

1 cup Julienned ham

4 large eggs

1 cup freshly grated Parmesan, plus more for serving

1 teaspoon garlic salt

Directions

Cook pasta in a pot of cold water until *al dente*.

Drain and add olive oil or butter.

Add the eggs, grated cheese, bacon and garlic salt.

Gnocchi

I started working at a bookstore in the mall in the early-90s. It was such a great job, for many reasons. Primarily because I would order my college books and apply my employee discount. Yup, I may have never taken calculus, but I have always done pretty well with personal finance, thank you very much!

There were no computers in the stores back in the day. I know, this is really hard to believe but it's true. I could write a book about all the stories I have from working at a bookstore.

The fact that there were no computers in the stores is important because we had microfiche. Boys and girls, it is now time to learn about microfiche, little blue pieces of plastic with tons of data written on it in super, teeny, tiny font. It was so small that you had to place the plastic into a machine that would magnify it on a lighted screen. Naturally, you had like a stack of fiche and often had to feed the machine several times in order to look up a title or author. Amazon didn't exist yet, and we didn't have smartphones at our sides at all times.

Working the information desk was always something of a gamble. It was great being able to help someone find the book they wanted, or to special order it for them. But it was much harder to help when a customer didn't know what he or she wanted. Even worse, sometimes random, old people would call us looking for books and of course, they didn't know the titles or authors.

Which brings me to the heart of this story.

One day an older woman called the store and was transferred to me while I was working the information desk. She was looking for an Italian chicken dumplings recipe that her husband had eaten one time someplace. It just so happened to be the holiday season, and I didn't really have time to look up vague chicken dumpling recipes in the back of a few hundred cookbooks. I suggested that she try several Italian cookbooks, but she asked me to check the books I recommended to see if they have the recipe for chicken dumplings that her husband might have tasted one time at some restaurant that he cannot recall. At least she thought it was a restaurant.

This same lady kept calling me back throughout the day, asking me if I had found her recipe. Keep in mind that I was about twenty years old at the time, and the extent of my cooking skills was limited to desserts, cereal, and pizza. I did own *The Starving Student's Cookbook* in paperback, (a curious size of four inches by eight inches) courtesy of my mom. Everyone had it in the dorms. It was right next to The Survival Guide with the red plaid print on the cover, sitting on the three-legged wood circular nightstand with a draped ruffle-y tablecloth. You know what I mean. Raise your hand. Okay.

I tried looking, but I couldn't find any Italian chicken dumpling recipes, so I told her as politely as I could that I hadn't found it. All the time I was wondering why she hasn't gone to her local library to find the book. I didn't exactly have all day to do her research while selling my book lovers card memberships. (I was very good at this. Seriously, I had sold the store record of memberships in a single day. Are you ready? 42. It's the meaning of life.)

But I became intrigued. This entree actually sounded really good. Maybe this lady's husband was on to something. But why couldn't I find it? I think I may have become a bit obsessed.

The next time she called to check up on me she said, "My husband just told me, it's not chicken! It's POTATO!"

"Geesh, lady!" I thought to myself. Out loud I said, "Okay, so that would be Gnocchi."

"YES!" she exclaims, "That was it!"

Big. Sigh. I had spent all day on this mission looking for a recipe that didn't exist! I ended up ordering her a cookbook containing a recipe for gnocchi. Of course, you would need a pasta-making machine for that...but did I tell her that? (I forget.)

No, I don't have a pasta-making machine at home, so I am not telling you how to make gnocchi here in this book. Unless -- well, I guess we could – like, wrap mashed potatoes in a wonton wrapper... YES!

Bless you, Gnocchi Lady.

Mashed Potato Spring Rolls with Bacon and Cheese

Ingredients:

- Mashed potatoes
- Wonton wrappers
- Cheddar cheese
- Bacon
- Sour cream

Directions:

Prepare mashed potatoes. I am not going to tell you how to make this part. (Use instant, I don't care.)

Place a dollop of creamy mashed potatoes inside a wonton wrapper.

Roll it like an egg roll.

Deep fry until crispy

Plate it in a row with criss-crossed rolls.

Garnish with shredded cheddar cheese and chopped bacon.

Serve with sour cream.

Juxtaposition Picnic

In the early to mid-90's, I was studying for a graduate degree in pastoral ministry with an emphasis in liturgical music. Yes, there are such fields of study and accredited universities offering such matters of study and subsequent degrees.

The movie Sister Act was in theaters and people were clapping along to a modernized Salve Regina in church like they do in the movie. I was young and inspired, having just found myself and my calling during my enjoyable undergraduate years. I happened upon an ad for this school, and I knew it was what I wanted to do. It was wonderful meeting so many other students, hanging out with them, and learning from and with them.

The visiting professors where delightful, famous men in the industry, and I will never forget the encouragement I received from Dr. Fred Moleck and Father Michael Joncas (who penned the Catholic staple of post-modern liturgical music: On Eagles' Wings which is in all the funerals and even in the movie Dead Man Walking.).

The most difficult thing for me about this experience was that the nuns didn't seem to like me.

I've since forgiven them. I mean, I was so demographically different, I don't think people knew how to react to me. I was 22 years old when I started (the youngest student in the program by a generation), and my curves were finally forming on my skinny frame (I know). And after surviving mononucleosis, I was delighted. I would wear cute, fashionable clothes that were not inappropriate, but the head nun actually asked me to wear shoulder pads and get a barrette for my hair if I should cantor/ lead the church in song.

One time, I decided to wear my favorite black and white polka-dot halter sundress to the summer picnic. It was a moderately long flowing skirt and, as is the nature of a halter-top, it was backless. And that was too much for the nuns. I am pretty sure one nun stood in my general vicinity and looked at the ground, shaking her head in dismay. If you have been in the shadow of a disapproving nun, you know what this is like. The black and white habit blocks the sun like a giant penguin and there is no escaping its enormous shadow, deserving or not.

Nearby, the Brazilian soccer team was practicing on the university fields, and their fans and family were enjoying a fantastically loud celebration picnic of their own. Soon the Brazilians were approaching me. I was a pretty young girl in an awesome dress! My conversational Spanish is very limited, and my Portuguese even more so, but we were communicating all the same. The fans had big drums strapped over one shoulder, and crossed the picnic lines to come serenade me with their drumming and dancing. Photographers offered me gifts, including a glossy photograph of the 1994 World Cup Team, with the athletes' signatures! I graciously accepted their offer and danced along with them.

I hope the nuns were watching.

Family Picnic Sandwich

with thanks to Uncle Dan Murphy

Uncle Dan invented this as a fun, easy way to prepare lunch for his family of six along camping trips. We think it's brilliant.

Ingredients(Housekeeping, Good , 2001)

> 1 round loaf Hawaiian bread
>
> Your favorite sandwich condiments
>
> Cheese slices- two kinds of cheese
>
> Ham slices and other deli meat slices

Instructions

> Slice the Hawaiian Loaf "top" off (lengthwise across the middle), You should have what looks like a giant muffin top and the bottom part which fits nicely into the pie tin it came in.
>
> Slice the "muffin top" again, lengthwise across the middle. Do the same for the bottom part. You should now have four layers of Hawaiian bread loaf.
>
> Make a giant four layer sandwich, as you would do for your favorite sandwich. Spread the mayo and/or mustard, layer the cheeses and meats. If you will be sharing this with little kids, leave the middle layer empty- so that there are two single-layer sandwiches. This will be easier for them.
>
> When you are all done, you should have a giant four-layer sandwich in the pie tin. Now, slice it like a pie: either in quarters or sixths. Now everyone can enjoy your favorite sandwich!

Holy Spirit Pot Luck

Armed with my Master's degree in Pastoral Ministries with an emphasis in Liturgical Music, I set about applying for music ministry positions. One parish that appealed to me was the Holy Spirit. The interview process had three levels. First, I would meet a hiring committee comprised of choir members, parishioners, and staff. Second, I would meet the choir and conduct an actual choir rehearsal. Third, I would lead the choir and community in song at an actual Mass. I was told that I was

one of three candidates. I even attended one Mass in which another candidate was "auditioning." (That was helpful. I saw her do some interesting things like actually conduct the congregation with a baton. No, thank you. This is California; most people haven't had music education in public schools since the 1970's. We don't conduct congregations with a baton! As if.)

The first meeting was in the parish office, which appeared to be a repurposed single family home. I was shown to a great room with a large dining table that sat about 14 people. I wasn't even able to tell who was the parish priest at first, since he was dressed in "civilian" clothes. I wore a black blazer, cream shell, and black and cream striped pencil skirt with black heels. I thought I did okay, and sure enough, I was called back for round two.

For round two, I conducted rehearsal for the choir and even said a prayer I had written. I thought it went well. A few members had lined up to speak with me afterwards, including the longtime parish pianist, Noel, who said to me, "I vote for you! You look like Linda Ronstadt!" Well, I had just spent all this time and money to get a master's degree in Pastoral Ministries with an emphasis in Liturgical Music, and here it seemed this wide-eyed woman would be selecting me solely on the basis of my resemblance to a 1970's singer. Sing with me, now: "I'm coming back, someday!" (You know I love you if you just sang that phrase in your head. Even more if you sang it out loud.) Anyway, round three happened, and soon I was hired.

The choir and the community were so welcoming to me, which was really affirming, as I had chosen their parish even though it was only a half-time position -- officially (but you know ministry is ministry and there's no such thing as part-time), and I had to get another full-time job working at the local Barnes & Noble Bookseller. But Noel and her family were particularly welcoming.

Noel was a spirited, creative soul who also worked at the IRS. Fascinating, right? She travelled worldwide with her husband, toting along paints, and using water from the local rivers and streams. She wanted to be my friend, even though I was the age of her own daughter. She'd invite me to ride along with her to the car wash so that we could get mochas in the wait-area café and talk. She invited me to dinner and parties at her home. We'd often provide music at back-to-back masses and sit at the piano bench together, huddling behind the music desk and whispering during the homilies. We had a system, where we could both play piano during the communion song, and each receive communion. I might receive communion first, then slide in next to her on the bench and start playing the left hand part while she got up on the other side. As she stood, I would take over the right hand piano part, too, and the effect was seamless. No one listening would know we had switched piano players mid-song.

Noel and I both were improvisational piano players, meaning we read the guitar chord symbols more than the actual notes. We don't really plan which accompanying notes we will play it sort of just happens. By the power of the Holy Spirit. "Isn't it wonderful?" she'd say when someone complimented her piano playing, "It's the Holy Spirit!"

Soon the time came to plan for the traditional end-of-year choir party. I suggested we have a sign-up sheet for what people would bring. She said, "Oh, no, we don't do that! Just let everybody bring what they want to bring. It always works out. It's a Holy Spirit Pot Luck!" But to the rest of us, it's just a pot luck, right? Anyway. There were far too many casseroles, so we set up everything in two phases, and called it dinner.

Sad to say, Noel passed away in 2010. She joined her oldest son in heaven. My own son is named after him. My daughter and I carry Noel's tradition of water coloring along our travels.

God Bless You, Noel.

Spinach Casserole

This is Noel's recipe for her casserole of choice.

Ingredients:

2 packages frozen spinach, cooked and drained well.

1 cup sour cream

½ cup grated Cheddar

½ cup grated Jackcheese

½ cup grated Parmesan

¼ cup chopped scallions

1 teaspoon Italian Herb seasoning

1 lb. ground beef

½ cup cheddar cheese

½ cup Monterey Jack cheese

12 mushroom caps

Directions:

Preheat oven to 350°.

Mix spinach together with sour cream, parmesan, and Italian herb seasoning. Set aside

Place mushroom caps cut side up in square casserole dish and spoon spinach around the edge of the casserole dish.

Sauté ground beef and put in the center of the dish. Top it all with scallions, ½ cup cheddar and ½ cup jack cheeses.

Cover. Bake for 25 minutes

Way Back Wednesday

During my freshman year, two friends and I entered an open mic contest at a local pub. We were underage but that didn't seem to matter at the time. They let the three of us in. I was not prepared for how rowdy it would be. Did I mention that we were all in the chapel choir? I recall vividly how I wore my pink turtleneck sweater and my big hair like something like a mix of Deanna Troi from *Star Trek the Next Generation* and Elaine from *Seinfeld*, complete with a big pink scrunchie. (It was still the 80's.)

The emcee was stirring the first act a nasty comedian. The second act was two dudes with guitars singing Bon Jovi's "Dead or Alive." The third act was made of two dudes lip-synching air guitar to Bon Jovi's "Dead or Alive". The crowd booed them off the stage. We three lowly and somewhat naïve freshmen stuck out like a sore thumb. I asked my friends several times if they wanted to bail and of course, they didn't want to leave.

When it was our turn, we performed my original piece, simply titled, "Love Song." Amazingly, the crowd quieted respectfully, as I began playing the introduction on the old, out-of-tune upright piano in the corner of this dark and dusty pub. As the composer, I had the unique advantage of substituting notes on the fly, as not all of the piano keys worked. I subbed an A in the bass line -- that's okay, I remember thinking, A-minor is close enough to C major. My two confident friends aced the duet, singing sweetly and dramatically and the crowd cheered respectfully.

We left the pub soon after our performance. We didn't even stay to see if we had won. It so wasn't our scene. Now whenever I hear "Dead or Alive" by Bon Jovi, I recall that night of uncertainty, with a smile.

Salami and Cheddar Wraps

Ingredients:

Flour Tortillas, plain or sundried-tomato tortilla wraps

Whipped Cream Cheese

Grated Cheddar Cheese

Deli Sliced Salami

Directions:

Spread cream cheese on tortillas. Sprinkle grated cheese evenly over cream cheese. Place sliced salami on top, like a pizza. Roll up and press lightly to secure. (The cream cheese should make everything stick.)

Slice in thirds on the diagonal, or, slice in one-inch increments to make "wheels" These look really colorful when displayed, and they are of course yummy.

Apple Butter Sandwich

(Another substitute for a boring sandwich)

Wheat bread

Spreadable cream cheese

Apple butter

You know what to do. It's like fluffer-nutters, only with cheese and apples, so you can pretend it is healthy. (It probably is a little bit healthier.)

Roast beef on ciabatta with sundried tomato ricotta pesto

(The bestest sandwich)

You can buy a tri-level dip at the big box stores in California. It is basically ricotta, pesto, and sun-dried tomatoes. If you do not have a Trader Joe's near you, you can buy the three items separately. You are just going to mix it all up together, anyway.

The ciabatta rolls are just a little bit fancier than your daily bread. It tells your audience (eaters) that this is a special occasion. If you were fortunate to find the premade dip, great, now mix it all together so that it is a kind of pink ricotta with pesto and sundried tomatoes sticking out. If you had to buy them separately, don't worry, just mix it all together. It looks the same.

Now spread the mix on the bread. Add slices of deli roast beef. That's it!

A Faithful Friend

Let me tell you about my friend Dani. Dani sat behind me in Honors English in high school. She has piercing green-grey eyes, dark curly hair, and gorgeous skin. We traded notes for our Religious Studies classes, just to compare. I knew she was a softball player and she knew I was in band. But we didn't really become friends until we went to college.

Something about carpooling to college, and you are bound to become lifelong friends. We were the only two Religious Studies majors in our entering freshmen class. People used to actually get us mixed up, due to the big curly hair (it was 1989). For many years, we would meet at restaurants and say to the host, I'm meeting someone who looks like me only she has green/brown eyes." And it would work, every time. I'd enter the restaurant, and the host would say, "Your friend is here! I'll take you to her."

Dani has a knack for always knowing the right thing to say. It is her unique perspective, as being the youngest in her family, but also growing up partly as an only child (as she was so much younger) and later when her niece came to live with them, Dani became like the oldest child. Dani is fiercely intelligent and extremely well-read, so her humor is spot-on.

During our collegiate years, Dani would sometimes withdraw and not want to talk to people. She would ask me to talk to the campus postman for her. So I would. We would approach the window and I'd be her proxy. If there was a question, I'd have to whisper to her and she'd whisper back. Probably the postman thought she spoke a foreign language, and I was her translator.

Even when our circles divided, we remained special friends. When one of her boyfriends broke up with her, she joined a gym. When mine broke up with me, I got mono for like a year. When my first child was diagnosed with Autism, she was sleep training her baby in a foreign country. I will always treasure our emails of support. It is having helped each other through these trying times that strengthens our bond. As it is written in Sirach 6:

> 14 Faithful friends are a sturdy shelter:
> whoever finds one has found a treasure.
> 15 Faithful friends are beyond price;
> no amount can balance their worth.
> 16 Faithful friends are life-saving elixir;
> and those who respect the Lord will find them.

I would do anything for her.

Dani has had so many interesting jobs and experiences. She was in *Rocky Horror Picture Show*, she's lived abroad in London and Brussels, and she was a field representative for a congresswoman. With her Master's Degree in Counseling Psychology and her talent for helping, it's only natural that she is now a Wellness Coach and Learning Center Coordinator/ Academic Coach. Dani is writing her first book and I can't wait!

Sautéed Cabbage with Bacon and Pecans

(Dani's Paleo-friendly recipe)

Ingredients:

4 slices of thick cut pastured bacon

2-3 cloves of minced garlic

1 head of chopped red cabbage.

Juice of 1 small lemon

Sea salt

Black pepper to taste

¼ cup of chopped pecans

Directions:

Fry 4 slices of thick cut pastured bacon in a large frying pan and remove when done.

Add 2-3 cloves of minced garlic to the bacon fat and heat until slightly soft.

Add 1 head of chopped red cabbage and sauté with garlic until soft. Add chopped bacon.

Squeeze in the juice of 1 small lemon, add sea salt and black pepper to taste.

In a separate pan, lightly toast ¼ cup of chopped pecans. Add to cabbage and mix.

Serve warm.

Rice, Rice, Baby

My mom had just called out to my helpful friend, "Bridget, Don't spill the rice!" when of course, Bridget turned toward my mom and in doing so, slipped her grip on the 40-pound bag of rice. Raw, uncooked rice grains scattered across the moss-green linoleum and into the corners of the 1970's décor kitchen, under the avocado refrigerator. And we laughed together.

It's very common to have a 40-pound bag of rice in Asian-Pacific Islander households. Rice is a staple. There are so many uses for rice, and not just in cooking. I once witnessed my mom use rice as an adhesive. She calls this "Guamanian know-how," which means creative, non-conventional problem-solving. She wanted to use an old postage stamp, but it had lost its stick. You place just one grain of rice on the corner of the envelope, place that postage stamp on top, then smash that grain with your thumb. Just smash it! Done.

I once dropped my cell phone into a creek and I tried the "rice trick" to dry it out. In an air-tight container, place the water-damaged phone in a bed of uncooked rice overnight. The grains absorb the moisture from the phone. I swear, this works. Although, I did have to go to the phone store and ask for their help removing a couple of grains from the adaptor orifice. (Oops.) Fortunately, it still worked, and none of my thousand-plus precious family photos were lost.

My daughter once made me a sweet penholder for Mother's Day --a flowered pen in a tiny flower pot filled with rice. I proudly displayed it on my cubicle ledge at work. Then one day, a friendly co-worker knocked it over and all the rice spilled into my desktop printer. I had to phone the printer maintenance dude and request a printer cleaning. What was the reason? He inquired. Uh, rice in my printer. From that point on, I was known as the girl with the rice in her printer.

Red Rice

Ingredients:

    Rice

    Achiote seeds (annatto)

    Water

    Rice cooker

    Onions, or onion powder

    Peas (optional)

Directions:

    Okay, the secret is in the spice. The Achiote seeds (English word is Annato) are the key. Place the seeds in a large bowl of water. Let the color from the seeds drain and color the water. This is where the magic happens. Drain the actual seeds out of your achiote water.

    If you are serious about this, get a separate rice cooker bowl. Henceforth this will be your dedicated "red rice" rice cooker bowl. I'm serious. Do it. You don't want to have your boss over for dinner one day and try to make white rice but it comes out a tinge orangish because you hadn't washed out all of the achiote residue. Right?

    Prepare the rice as you would normally. For persons of Asian Pacific Islander descent, this means use your thumb. Am I right? I just love it when these nonconventional traditions really work.

I have a particular abhorrence for onions, so I would use onion powder. No slimy worms in my rice, thank you very much!

Remembering Grandma Santos

I was so fortunate to have my grandma living with us when I was a young girl. I loved her then, and I have even greater respect and admiration for her now. She was with us for all of our special occasions. She let my beloved cat cuddle near her, even though she wasn't particularly fond of cats. She was so warm, and genuinely loving, as my relatives from Guam are. She always made sure to snuggle and hug my sister and I when it was the other sister's birthday. And she could fry Vienna sausage like no one else.

I cannot even imagine the hardships she endured, growing up on Guam in the early twentieth century. Her island was captured by Japan during World War II happened, and her family was forced to march between villages along with the other native islanders. Her young son became separated from her during the march, and wasn't reunited with the family for a day. Can you even imagine?

She sure made me feel special and loved, and I know she did the same for her other twenty-six grandchildren. She walked us to the park at the top of the hill so we could play on the playground. She wore a lace shawl over her head, reminiscent of how Catholic women had to cover their hair in church in pre-Vatican II times. I still remember the shiny black patent leather Mary Jane's with the big fat buckle that she gave me one year. (Maybe that's why I have always loved Mary Janes!)

Sometimes when I find a food truck now I will ask them to prepare a meal that I remember my grandma cooking for us. It is basically eggs and rice, with fried Vienna sausage. Then I douse it with soy sauce. (You know you are an Asian Pacific Islander if you keep a bottle of soy sauce in your desk at work!) The likes and loves start pouring in when I post a picture of my meal on Facebook or Instagram! Many of my family, friends, and followers remember this comfort meal.

I remember the Tejas that Grandma cooked for us. Tejas is short for Titiyas, the traditional flatbread. I remember watching her making this in our home, when I was growing up. She'd give me a little of the dough and I could make my own tiny tejas. If I concentrate on the memory, I can almost smell her presence -- Rose Milk hand lotion and Cheerios. It's wonderful to now watch my own children make tejas with my mom.

I miss you, Grandma.

Titiyas

Flatbread from Guam

(pronounced tih-TEE-jus or TEE-jus for short.)

My grandmother would make this from memory, without ever measuring. My mom studied her process and came up with these measurements.

Ingredients:

1 cube butter

½ cup sugar

4 cups flour

1 tablespoon baking powder

1 cup milk (or coconut milk, per my mom)

Directions:

Cream butter and sugar.

In the same bowl, pour in the flower and baking powder.

Stir just the top dry ingredients, before mixing all together with the milk.

Mix until contents form a ball.

Separate into five balls.

Flatten each ball and roll between two sheets of waxed paper with rolling pin.

Cook on griddle one to two minutes each side. There is no need to use oil/spray on the pan because of the butter.

Makes five large tejas.

Great with cheese and ham. (Even spam.)

Fina'denne

(Literally means from the pepper)

Ingredients:
- Soy sauce
- White vinegar (sauce to vinegar 1:1 ratio)
- Lemon juice
- Green onions
- White onions
- Hot chili peppers, as much as you can stand

Directions:
- Mix together and pour over rice or meat

Chicken Kelaguen

Kelaguen is a Chamorro dish from the Northern Mariana Islands eaten as a side dish or as a main course. You can kelaguen any meat; actually, I have seen photos of octopus kelaguen. But I am not going near that stuff. I will present to you the traditional method, as well as my more modern approach.

Traditional Chamorro Ingredients:

Uncooked steak OR barbequed chicken

Juice of one lemon

grated fresh coconut

sliced onion

salt

red hot "boonie" pepper

Directions:

Clean and chop the chicken into tiny pieces. Douse with lemon juice. The "heat" (acidity) of the lemon juice is what cooks the meat.

Mix coconut, onion, vinegar and salt with chicken.

Garnish with small red hot pepper.

Have a glass of milk on hand. This is how we identify the Haolies (non-natives): those who cannot handle the pepper. Makes the Haolies cry, and then they drink water and it makes it worse. Be nice to your Haolie friends. Have milk ready.

Contemporary Ingredients:

Cooked chicken breast

Lemon juice, bottled is okay

shredded coconut (packaged is okay)

onion powder

rice wine vinegar

salt

Directions:

Chop the chicken breast into tiny pieces. Douse with lemon juice.

Mix coconut, onion, vinegar and salt with chicken.

Simple Gifts

Sometimes the most basic things are the best. You know what I mean. Sunrise. Sunset. A kiss on the cheek. A sweet thank you from a child. Stuffed mushrooms. Peanut Butter Balls.

Peanut Butter Balls is one creation that is not even truly a recipe. Equal parts peanut butter and marshmallow crème. Mix it together. Get sticky. Roll in to balls. Refrigerate for thirty minutes. Done.

See what I mean? What are some of your simply divine blessings? I'd love to know. Please visit my blog at https://www.denisederrico.wordpress.com and leave me a comment!

Stuffed Mushrooms

Ingredients:

2 (12 ounce) packages white button mushrooms,

1 (8 ounce) brick cream cheese

1 (8 ounce) packages sausage

Garlic, Italian spices to taste

Directions:

Preheat oven to 350° Fahrenheit.

Separate caps and stems while cleaning the mushrooms.

Start cooking the sausage in frying pan, at a medium to medium/high temperature.

While the sausage is cooking, put the cream cheese into a mixing bowl so it can soften and mince the stem pieces.

Spice the sausage, to taste.

Just before the sausage is done, add the mushroom stem pieces and finish cooking.

Drain off the excess grease and add the sausage/stem mixture into the cream cheese.

Mix together well using a wooden spoon.

Set the caps into a 13x9 casserole dish

Fill the caps with the cream cheese/sausage/stem mix.

Add a small amount of water to the bottom of the pan, just enough to cover the bottom.

Bake for 30 to 45 minutes, or until the tops are crusty and the mushrooms have turned dark.

Scoop them out of the pan with a slotted spoon and serve warm.

Reflections

It never ceases to amaze me how storytelling is part of the story. Somebody somewhere sometime thought of an idea and it is very likely that somebody else somewhere else some other time thought of something similar. But one's life experience and environment color one's perception, so the story may be different. It's the same with music, and with recipes.

My story is that I come from a mixed culture family. So l like to mix things up. I sense that certain dynamics "go" together- even when others might not perceive the connections immediately. I am a mix of Caucasian and Pacific Islander, not quite fully fitting into either group. I believe this has given me a unique perspective. I have just enough light and just enough dark that no one can figure out what I truly am, rather everybody seems to think I am whatever they are. Which is kind of cool. I once met my features twin- and she was of a completely different ethnicity from the opposite part of the world! Also, being of mixed heritage has given me a passion for combining the unexpected: Harry Potter and Autism, labyrinths and the Enneagram, fairy tales and 80's music, etc. I am both spiritual and religious, I am both liberal and conservative, I am both an alto and a soprano, I like both Star Trek and Star Wars, I am both a zip-liner and a bookworm.

I love being unique. I love being different. Go against the grain! You just gotta do what works for you. Change my recipes! In fact, I dare you.

Thank you for reading!

References:

Housekeeping, Good. (2001). *The Good Housekeeping Illustrated Cookbook: America's Bestselling Step-by-Step Cookbook with More Than 1,400 Recipes.* New York: Hearst.

Kimmel, M. a. (2000). *Mommy Made and Daddy Too! (Revised): Home Cooking for a Healthy Baby & Toddler.* New York: Bantam .

Kondo, M. (2014). *The Life-Changing Magic of Tidying Up: The Japanese Art of Decluttering and Organizing.* Ten Speed Press.

For the Reader

I hope you have enjoyed *Dee's Dishes*. I wrote this book for you, so that you would think about sharing your own stories and recipes, too. Let's Dish! I bet you have recipes you'd like to share and stories you'd like to tell. What is your story?

I know my own story is still developing. I also have more stories to tell, including the story I believe I was meant to write. Stay tuned for news about *The Other Side of the Ocean*.

As an author, I love feedback. You are the reason I am writing. So, tell me what you liked, what you loved, and even what you hated. I would love to hear from you. You can write me at derricodenise@gmail.com or visit my website at www.denisederrico.wordpress.com.

Finally, I need to ask a favor. If you are so inclined, I'd love a review of *Dee's Dishes*. Loved it, hated it—I'd just enjoy the feedback. Reviews can be tough to come by these days. You, the reader, have the power to make or break a book. I invite you to take a moment to leave a review on amazon.com.

https://www.amazon.com/Denise-Dwyer-DErrico/e/B00R54XLXM/ref=sr_ntt_srch_lnk_1?qid=1483479634&sr=8-1

Thank you so much for reading Dee's Dishes and spending time with me.

Peace,

Denise

About the Author

Denise Dwyer D'Errico is a poet, author, musician, wife, mother, and a seeker of her own truth. She has written and self-published a poetry collection entitled *A Maze in Grace* and contributed to *Teaching with Harry Potter: Essays on Classroom Wizardry from Elementary School to College*, edited by Valerie E. Frankel.

Denise has over twenty years of experience as a liturgical musician, as cantor, piano accompanist, and music director of adult choirs, children's choirs, musicals, and handbell choirs. She is the composer of "Be Still," a liturgical choral piece published by the leading church music publisher GIA. She has also provided piano, vocal, and music theory instruction for children and adults. She has spoken to audiences on parenting and autism awareness. Denise has particular interest in illustrating harmony among seemingly unrelated subjects.

And she really loves crème brûlée.

Printed in Great Britain
by Amazon